I am so grateful Tom and Jan wrote this book. There is no better couple I know who can teach the strength of marriage and family than this dynamic duo. My wife, Pam, and I have learned so much from watching and listening to them. You will grow in your relationships if you read and heed the wise words on these pages.

—Brady Boyd
Senior pastor, New Life Church
@pastorbrady

In this book Tom and Jan Lane uncover the frontlines of conflict in so many marriages—the power struggle of personalities. From their forty-plus years of marriage, Tom and Jan know that the only winners of these relational battles are the couples who learn to love each other's differences, to forgive each other's wounds, and to unite in their dependence on God's grace. This book moves beyond the love and respect required to make a marriage work and takes us to hope and healing.

—Chris Hodges
Senior pastor, Church of the Highlands
Author, *Fresh Air and Four Cups*

Tom and Jan have opened up their lives and marriage to us to learn from in this book. Their story sounds so familiar to those we minister to at The Hideaway Experience. Reading this book will open the eyes of so many couples who struggle with their differences. What a great way marriage allows God to begin transforming you individually and then as a couple.

—Steve and Rajan Trafton
Cofounders and operators, The Hideaway Experience

Often books dealing with the subject of marriage are not relatable or respectful to both husband and wife. Thankfully, Tom and Jan Lane have crafted a book that allows for both parties to feel understood, utilizing material that is tailored to respect the individuals as well as the institution of marriage. Because of their approach this is one of the most relevant, authentic, and applicable marriage books I have read in my career as a therapist and educator. The sound, biblical concepts combined with personal transparency allow the reader to relate and find the root of the issues they may be facing. I feel strongly that this book holds the recipe for marriage success, personal growth, and spiritual freedom.

—DR. CASSIE REID, LPC-S, PHD
FOUNDER, CASSIE REID COUNSELING
PROFESSOR OF BIBLICAL COUNSELING, THE KING'S UNIVERSITY

Power struggles! Every couple has them and no one wins. Tom and Jan Lane teach us how to grow through them and give us practical help for our own marriages. You will love their honest, open transparency. I urge you to read this book!

—NANCY HOUSTON
ASSOCIATE PASTOR, MARRIAGE & FAMILY MINISTRIES
GATEWAY CHURCH

In my twenty years of marriage ministry, helping reserved men step up to lead their wives effectively has been the single most difficult problem I have faced. Now I have the perfect resource to assist those couples. Tom and Jan Lane unlock the mystery of marriage harmony between passive men and assertive wives. Their wisdom, insight, and practical application will change your life. This is a must-read.

—TRAVIS TURNER
FOUNDER, DIVINE ROMANCE MINISTRIES INC.
AUTHOR OF *THE FAMILY QUARTERBACK*

STRONG
WOMEN
and the *men*
WHO LOVE THEM

TOM & JAN LANE

GATEWAY
CREATE
PUBLISHING

Most CHARISMA HOUSE BOOK GROUP products are available at special quantity discounts for bulk purchase for sales promotions, premiums, fund-raising, and educational needs. For details, write Charisma House Book Group, 600 Rinehart Road, Lake Mary, Florida 32746, or telephone (407) 333-0600.

STRONG WOMEN AND THE MEN WHO LOVE THEM
    by Tom and Jan Lane
Published by Gateway Create Publishing
Gateway Create Publishing
700 Blessed Way
Southlake, TX 76092
www.gatewaycreate.com

Scripture quotations marked THE MESSAGE are from *The Message: The Bible in Contemporary English*, copyright © 1993, 1994, 1995, 1996, 2000, 2001, 2002. Used by permission of NavPress Publishing Group.

Cover design by Lisa Rae McClure
Design Director: Justin Evans

Visit the author's website at www.TomLaneBooks.com.

International Standard Book Number: 978-1-62998-592-3

Some names, places, and identifying details with regard to stories in this book have been changed to help protect the privacy of individuals who may have been involved or had similar experiences.

15 16 17 18 19 — 98765432
Printed in the United States of America

Gateway Create gratefully acknowledges the partnership of Charisma House in distributing this book.

This book is dedicated to our parents, Jim and Joyce Lane, and Dean and Dorothy Frazier. Their own commitment to love and to each other has given us a model to follow and a foundation to launch from in our marriage. The legacy of their lives and relationships lives on in new generations of our children and grandchildren. We honor and thank you for your commitment, faithfulness, and love!

CONTENTS

FOREWORD

❧

THE FIRST TIME MY WIFE, DEBBIE, AND I WENT to dinner with Tom and Jan Lane, we got a glimpse of their different personalities. We were going around the table ordering our food, and when I gave my order, Jan said, "Great! I've been wanting to try that!" I looked at her and said, "You better order some for yourself, because you're not getting any of mine." She just laughed, and at the same time I was thinking, "I'm serious. You're not getting any of my food!" But sure enough, when the food came out, she reached over with her fork and took a bite!

I was rather taken aback when it happened, but later I realized it's normal for couples to be opposites of each other. I had expected Jan to be more like Tom, whom I had met before that night and even played golf with on several occasions, yet he is the exact opposite. He's a strategic leader who's contemplative and thinks through things carefully. Then there's Jan. She has a vivacious and outgoing personality and is fun and bubbly—always the life of the party. She's never met a stranger, and she certainly isn't afraid to eat off a new friend's plate! When it comes to Tom and Jan, the saying "opposites attract" couldn't be more true.

Really, their situation isn't unusual. Couples are like puzzle pieces. They are all different sizes and shapes, yet they fit together perfectly. It's that way with Tom and Jan. I like to say that they're a match made in heaven, but thunder and lightning are also made in heaven. They have some opposite characteristics of their personalities that, without Christ, could have caused their marriage to fail; yet they also have similarities that have allowed them to have a strong connection with each other.

After being in ministry for more than thirty years, I've seen this dynamic in many marriages. One spouse has a tendency to be quieter, more passive, and contemplative, while the other has a tendency to be outgoing, think out loud, talk a lot, and, in some ways, dominate the conversation. When the man is outgoing and the woman is quiet, their relationship fits nicely within our views and expectations of what marriage should look like. But when the personalities are reversed, the man is often viewed as a weak leader who is dominated by his stronger, more aggressive wife. Many times, we'll try to change their personalities to fit within the "ideal model" instead of embracing the various ways God made them to interact with each other.

You may be the complete opposite of your spouse, but it's actually good because it's the way God created you. He created you in His likeness, and when you come together as one, you make up the image of God. A strong woman and a quiet man aren't doomed for marital destruction. Their marriage can actually be great when they appreciate and understand each other's strengths, yield them to Christ, and make a commitment to grow in their areas of weakness. We can't just say, "That's just the way I am." We do need to allow God to work and change some areas of our lives.

I've known Tom and Jan for more than twenty-five years. Our friendship goes back a long way, and I've personally seen the principles they write about in this book succeed in their lives. They have one of the best marriages of any couple I know, not only because they're so perfectly matched, but because they've learned to appreciate each other's strengths and haven't been afraid to work on their weaknesses.

My hope is that as you read this book, you'll ask the Lord to show you any of the areas in your life that need to be yielded to Him, and then surrender those to God.

—ROBERT MORRIS
FOUNDING SENIOR PASTOR, GATEWAY CHURCH
DALLAS/FORT WORTH, TEXAS
BEST-SELLING AUTHOR, *THE BLESSED LIFE*,
FROM DREAM TO DESTINY, *THE GOD I NEVER KNEW*,
AND *THE BLESSED CHURCH*

PREFACE

❦

OMETIME AGO I (TOM) WAS TALKING WITH MY friend Jimmy Evans of MarriageToday about ministering to marriages. Jimmy has been my best friend for more than thirty years, and we share a passion for helping marriages. I have been on the board of MarriageToday from its beginning in 1994 and served as the chief operating officer of the ministry until September 2004.

Jimmy and Karen have ministered to marriages from the perspective of a dominant man and a passive woman. They have imparted principles for marriage success to millions of couples through books, TV, and seminars. Jan and I have been privileged to help and support them in that effort. And we have done that while working to build a vibrant marriage of our own.

One day Jimmy said to me, "I know a book that you and Jan ought to write." I said, "Really? What book is that?" He said we should write a book on marriage and call it *Dominant Women and Passive Men.* In one sentence he was able to offend both Jan and me!

For the sake of argument, I asked him to explain, and he went on to say his marriage is one that involves a dominant man and a passive woman but that he estimates up to half of all marriages are made up of dominant women and passive men. He said that in all the years he has known us and observed our marriage interactions, our marriage is the healthiest reflection of that type of marriage makeup.

He said, "If you would share what you have learned, it would help a lot of couples with their marriages."

That conversation became the catalyst for this book. It is our honor to share with you what we have learned and applied in our forty-plus years of marriage with the dynamic of an aggressive woman and a passive man in the hope that, if that's the same dynamic you face, we can give you encouragement and provide you with tools to help you build the marriage of your dreams.

INTRODUCTION

❧ Tom ❧

ROMANTIC THOUGHTS OF RELATIONAL BLISS have their roots in fairy tales. Cinderella, the attractive young woman who was mistreated by her mean stepmother and stepsisters, finds help through a fairy godmother. A pumpkin is turned into a coach, mice become tailors and coachmen, and Cinderella captures the heart of the prince at the ball. The story ends with the declaration that they married and lived happily ever after. We think, "If that can happen to Cinderella, why not to me?" We need "the rest of the story," as Paul Harvey used to say.

The greatest joy and fulfillment in marriage comes as the result of two hearts becoming one. Achieving this result involves a process that allows the uniqueness of the two individuals to be blended together. The expression of each person's gifts enhance the relationship as each one values and supports the other without one person dominating or repressing the other.

Our own perspective is uniquely individual and when blended with our spouse's, it gives a greater perspective to life's circumstances and reflects the partnership God designed for marriage. This is the process that produces the fullest results from blending our lives together into one focus, one purpose, and one heart with multiple reflections as it produces fulfillment and happiness for both parties in the marriage. This is God's perfect design.

The truth is, not every woman is Cinderella and not every man is Prince Charming! Every person is uniquely created, so there are as many personality dynamics as there are people in the world. When it comes to building a marriage partnership, every relationship is one-of-a-kind, meaning we do not uniformly reflect the people depicted on screen. When two different personalities come together, they create a unique combination that must be considered in order to grow the relationship. Each couple has to contend with their differences, all with the aim of discovering what it means, in their relationship, to become uniquely one—reflecting the partnership God designed us to experience in marriage.

As we build a partnership with our spouse, there is one aspect of our lives regardless of our individuality that all couples must address. We must address the way we communicate, deal with conflict, and make decisions to ensure that both parties are honored and represented in the relationship.

When a woman is confident, gifted, and strong, her aggressive actions and reactions may come across as dominant, controlling, or even offensive. When a man is confident but reflective and nonconfrontational, his slowness to engage can come across as passive, weak, and uncaring. If a couple with these tendencies wants to build a deep and satisfying marriage, they need to address the issues that crop up through these varied expressions of their personalities.

The passive husband is disposed toward avoiding conflict in an effort to create peace and harmony at any price. His approach makes communication less direct and more subtle, as he believes that peace and harmony can be achieved with less emotional friction. For an outgoing wife, this approach is unclear, evasive, and confusing, leaving her perplexed about her next step. The aggressive woman's nature is to engage her husband on issues that impact their lives with little regard for peace and harmony. She is single-minded in her pursuit of connection and finding solutions to the circumstances being faced in the relationship. Her approach makes this process focused and direct and confrontational when needed, in an effort to arrive at an immediate result—all of which causes her passive husband to back away from an encounter with her.

Each approach is successful on its own, but when partnered in marriage, the individual approaches can become adversarial. Each person seeks their own method for solution and opposes the other's, leading to frustration, misunderstanding, invalidation, and division. It is a balancing act that takes awareness, commitment, and determination.

In this book Jan and I are bringing our marriage experiences along with our pastoral counseling observations together to help men and women who, like us, are dealing with the dynamics of an aggressive, confident, strongly gifted, and opinionated wife and a strongly gifted, opinionated, confident, yet more passively reserved husband. In each chapter we share stories with you that reveal our perspectives, experiences, and struggles as we have built our marriage over more than forty years. We share how we have dealt with the dynamics of a strong woman and a reflective man on our way to building a marriage that is mutually fulfilling, satisfying, and representative of a partnership that includes and represents God's plan for marriage.

The temptation with this dynamic is to build coping mechanisms to deal with our differences rather than address them. Believe us, we get that. But rather than build coping mechanisms that would allow us to "get by" or ignore and deny our frustrations until they became so toxic that we can no longer stand each other, we choose to act with faith and diligence each day to address issues in our personal lives and as a couple that produce barriers in our marriage. We refuse to allow bitterness or unforgiveness to become a part of our relationship, as we know the fruit of bitterness and unforgiveness ultimately destroys each person and the marriage by ruining the loving commitment the two people share.

Over the years of our marriage it has been our mutual, determined commitment to make our marriage reflect all that God intended when He brought us together. The effort that is needed to build a mutually satisfying relationship is not revealed in the fairy-tale statement, "They lived happily ever after." We have worked hard to develop the respect, honor, and connection that has contributed to the fruitful relationship and connection we enjoy today.

It takes consistent, diligent, selfless effort coupled with grace and forgiveness to bring it about, but we can tell you it is worth it.

We have been unwilling to settle for less than what we believe is God's intended best in our marriage, and we want the same for you. We believe God's best reflects a relational partnership that includes Him at the center of the relationship and our partnership with Him to produce His purposes on earth. The strength of our desire for that kind of marriage has provided fuel for our commitment and has propelled us to find answers to the frustrations we have encountered over the years, and we hope you are inspired to strive for a similar vision in your own marriage.

While our marriage is not perfect—we are still growing and learning—we are committed to each other, we love each other, and we have learned to successfully blend our very different personalities and perspectives into a happy, satisfying marriage. We share what we have learned here with you in the confidence that God will help you apply it to your situation in just the way you need to strengthen, encourage, and connect your lives in a marriage that satisfies all your dreams and desires!

Chapter 1

UNCOVERING THE PASSIVE MAN

❧ TOM ❧

IT WAS MY NINTH-GRADE YEAR AND I WAS BARELY in my teens. I was assigned a seat in study hall next to a cute girl named Jan Frazier. She was full of life and so much fun. She was vocal, outgoing, and friends with everyone. This combination of her outgoing personality and the way she expressed herself got her in trouble regularly with our study hall teacher. Her constant socializing and her spunky attitude toward his oversight was more than he could handle some days. I think Jan spent more time in a chair facing a corner of the room than she did sitting next to me in productive study. In almost every one of her responses to life, she was different from me. She was an enigma to me—so fun, vibrant, and attractive, but also borderline disrespectful with her attitude and opinions. My perspective of Jan's situation was that she needed a better way of relating to authority.

Our study hall friendship eventually developed into a dating relationship and later into a marriage commitment. As our marriage progressed, I made an internal decision to take Jan's quirkiness on as my personal improvement project. I wanted to harness the life and energy she demonstrated into a more "productive" expression toward our friends, the authority figures in her life, and in her expressions toward me. I felt I could help her temper the strength of her responses and turn them into expressions that were more winsome and easier to receive.

The friction I felt between us was the strength of Jan's extroverted personality versus my relational diplomacy and tact. The stage was set for a wrestling match of perspectives, with marital harmony and purpose as the grand prize. But I had no idea all that would be involved in this match of personality, perspective, and power. I thought this would be a quick, easy fix on our way to marital bliss—yet on my way to fixing Jan, I uncovered issues about myself. At times it was difficult to tell if I was wrestling with Jan or the personal issues in my own life that impacted our relationship. What's more, it felt as if I was losing the wrestling match. It was hard to believe that the reason I was losing—and that the reason a quick victory had eluded me—might be more related to me and my issues than hers!

It took me much longer than it should have to recognize and acknowledge that my kind and diplomatic style of relating had a dark, unhealthy side. While it had the effect of making people feel good and often helped to defuse or avoid conflict, it produced dishonesty and ultimately allowed barriers of disconnection to be erected in my relationship with Jan. That is where my side of our story begins. It was not an easy process for me to uncover and accept the passive-aggressive underbelly of my "diplomatic," people-pleasing style of relating, but such discovery and self-examination was required for the health of our marriage.

WHAT IS PASSIVITY, REALLY?

Is the term *passive-aggressive* offensive to you? It is to me. I resisted identifying myself as passive-aggressive, and I denied, argued, and contended just short of fighting with any attempt by others to put that label on me. I associated passivity with negative terms like *wimp, loser, sissy,* and *mommy's boy,* and I wanted nothing to do with those descriptions. As I saw it, being passive meant being nonaggressive, weak, and without direction in life. I thought that passive people are the ones who are told what to do and how to think. As Scott Wetzler says in his book *Living With the Passive-Aggressive Man:*

> The term "passive aggressive" was first coined during World War II by an Army psychiatrist, Colonel William Menninger, who had been trained to deal with strong negative reactions to military life. Menninger recognized that the military is structured for uniformity and compliance, where individual choice, opinion or expertise does not change the rules, where you are obliged to suspend the determination of your own destiny. He noticed that while [some] men thrived under this rigorous institutional structure, others perished and protested...To deal with enforced change and cope with the lack of opportunity for personal choice, these soldiers resisted, ignored orders, withdrew or simply wanted to flee. Menninger labeled this resistance "passive-aggression" and described it as "an immaturity reaction.[1]

Passive-aggression is not a reflection of personality as much as it is a reaction to circumstances a person is experiencing. This tendency can be influenced by personality type, but even more it can be developed as a method of reacting to circumstances that make an individual feel overwhelmed and out of control with little or no option to determine the outcome. If a man concludes that his position is weak, threatened, or powerless to influence or change the circumstances around him and he acts with hidden, subtle resistance, his behavior is passive-aggressive. This response is developed as a pattern toward dominating authority and is often a reflection of performance thinking and the fear of failure or rejection.

Most people who relate passively within relationships have a hard time identifying themselves as passive. Here are six indicators of passivity to help you identify if this is your style of relating within relationships:

1. Inability to openly and honestly share your feelings

2. Punitive, retaliatory style of fighting or responding to disagreement

3. Low self-esteem and a people-pleasing personality

4. Avoidance of conflict until it is the last resort

5. Hidden, uncommunicated expectations or assumed conditions for the response from others

6. A victim mentality

Anyone can have one of these indicators and not be considered passive in the way they relate in their relationships. However, if these indicators are part of a man's regular reaction to his wife and they are coupled with times of emotional explosion or subtle resistance to her, that is a good bet that his behavior reflects passive-aggressive fruit.

Furthermore, confusion has developed regarding the way real men are supposed to act. As Wetzler says:

> Thirty years ago, men asserted their machismo by confrontation. If a man wanted something, and fought for it—this was called aggression, and it was sanctioned by society. The art of diplomacy, the use of tact, the role of mediator who smoothed the rough edges and defused serious conflict was a kind of passivity more characteristic of the traditional feminine role.[2]

It is hard for men to know how to fulfill their God-given responsibilities in a way that is consistent with their nature. John Eldredge also wrote about this dilemma in his book *Wild at Heart.*

The effort to avoid conflict can become so extreme that it is as unhealthy to a relationship as an emotional or physical abuse that seeks to establish the dominance of one person over another. Both extremes produce dysfunctional behavior that must be addressed and overcome. All forms of unhealthy behavior, if unchecked, lead to unhappiness, hopelessness, and ultimately disconnection between two individuals who were once very much in love.

As I have already explained, passivity relates to how you respond to circumstances of disagreement or conflict. The passive man seeks to avoid conflict so completely that he will deny his true feelings, burying them deep in his spirit, and go to extreme lengths to camouflage the nature of his emotions through denial. The *American Heritage Dictionary* describes *passive* as "receiving or subjected to an action without responding or initiating an action in return; accepting or submitting without objection or resistance; submissive."[3] In other words, passive behavior is a disconnected response to circumstances of disagreement or conflict.

Passivity can affect all types of friendships and working relationships. But when there is passive expression in a marriage, the other partner is left with no connection point, as the passive partner is not really showing up, so the depth of the relationship is stunted. Furthermore, when the passive partner's expression is linked with subtle aggression designed to resist the other person, not only is there nothing to connect the two of them, but the relationship is also systematically undermined. Passive-aggressive behavior is never more damaging then when it operates between a husband and wife.

Rarely have I seen two people with the same strength of personality come together in marriage. Passive men often marry aggressive women. Passive women often marry aggressive men. Through marriage counseling and my personal involvement with marriage ministry for more than twenty years, I know there are a large number of marriages that involve men who have adopted a passive-aggressive style of responding to circumstances when they feel powerless, feel they are at risk of rejection, or fear they will fail to meet the expectations of their wives. A marriage made up of a man with passive-aggressive tendencies and a woman with a strong or assertive personality has to overcome the negative influence of these characteristics to successfully build the marriage partnership God intended.

My resistance to being labeled a passive man and my unwillingness to identify my responses as passive-aggressive were, in my mind, completely justified responses. The terms and images those ideas created in my mind did not describe me. I am outgoing, competitive, and aggressive in pursuing things I set my mind on. I am expressive in my personality. How could I be called passive? I was convinced those who labeled me as passive were not thinking right. Furthermore, I found many men who were similar in their resistance, men who would refuse pastoral counseling because they feared being labeled, misunderstood, or branded by such a description.

Here is the reality I found: denial of the diagnosis does not cure the disease. Overcoming a passive-aggressive relational style requires an honest look at ourselves and the influences that have impacted our development. When men relate to their wives through passive-aggressive means, this clouds their honesty, hides expectations, and erects barriers that limit the depth of intimacy in their relationship.

My goal is to help you see passive-aggressive behavior in a different light. I want to expose the destructive power of this method of responding and help you see how it is limiting intimacy in your marriage. I hope to help you accept what others may have already identified in you and then lead you to an understanding of the thinking that lies behind your passive-aggressive responses.

Again, when I speak of passivity, I am speaking in relation to a behavior pattern, not a personality type. Some personalities are more laid back than others. While it is true that certain personalities lend themselves to passivity more easily than others, every personality type can display an aversion to conflict or, for various reasons, can feel controlled to the point of concluding they have no way to change or influence their circumstances, which creates conditions for passive-aggressive behavior and its detrimental influence on relational development.

Building a healthy marriage takes many tools relating to communication, forgiveness, and conflict resolution. Resolving conflict in relationships, especially in marriage, is not about winning or your drive for accomplishment. Neither is it about the importance of aggressively pursuing items of personal interest. Resolving conflict in marriage is about protecting a platform for deeper connection to your wife.

THE CAR INCIDENT

In the early years of our marriage I worked as a sales representative for a wholesale paper distribution company. In my sales capacity I made calls on customers to solicit orders for products that my company stocked and sold. The company gave me a car allowance that allowed me to purchase and use my own car for company business.

When I felt like the time had finally come to trade in our car for another one, I went looking for a car to replace the aging, high-mileage car I was driving, and I found one. I had some preliminary discussions about price with the salesman but told him I wanted my wife to see the car before I decided. I knew that an important buying decision like this needed Jan's agreement. However, when I went home and told Jan I had been looking for a car to replace the one I had been driving, she was shocked. As she processed her shock, it seemed she was resisting my desire to change vehicles. I was frustrated and put off by the barrage of questions she threw my way.

I finally convinced her to come with me to the dealership to check out the car. This would be the car I would drive for making calls on my customers. This perspective led me to select a plain, no frills, "meat and potatoes" salesman's car. It was a white Chevrolet Malibu with blue cloth seats and nothing electric or fancy. Jan hated it! There was nothing, not one thing, she liked about it.

Unfazed, I went to work to present my perspective and convince her that this was the car we needed and the one I wanted. I had expected when she came with me to the dealership that she would look at the car and simply give her approval. However, she wanted to engage in the process of the purchase. This put me in a panic. I interpreted her participation as an affront to my leadership. I felt she wanted to get the salesman in her grasp and squeeze him for a better price, taking out her frustration with me on him. I was concerned she wanted to work him for every penny she could, and I felt she would not be at all concerned that she might offend him with what I considered her brash way of relating.

I concluded all this without talking openly with Jan about any of these feelings or concerns. It seemed like a perfect time for me to help her learn a new way by showing her a gentler, diplomatic, winsome way to conduct business. During our negotiation, I (figuratively) stood between Jan and the salesman. As we came to a decision, I thought it was a mutually agreed upon decision, but it wasn't. The salesman was pleased, I was pleased, but Jan was not pleased. She was hurt and furious.

The problem was that I was clueless as to how the process had violated and invalidated her. I was more interested in being diplomatic with the salesman and leaving the dealership with him as my friend than I was in partnering with my wife in a decision for the benefit of me and our family. My people-pleasing diplomacy had undermined the relational connection I desired with my wife. I was clueless to the impact of its effect.

In a side note that reflects the humor of God, when we got the license plates for the car, the combination of letters and numbers read like this: *UKA-763*. The first time Jan saw the plate on the car, she said the plate called the car "yuk-a"! We dubbed the car Yuk-a the whole time we owned it. This was God's reminder to me of the ugly underbelly of my diplomatic way of relating and the hurtful barriers that passive-aggressive tendencies erect in marriage.

How Passivity Undermined Us

I was fully convinced that my avoidance of conflict with Jan was a godly expression of my love and that it was the right way—and biblical way—to keep harmony in our relationship. I often hid my true feelings from her aggressive, passionate expressions regarding issues and circumstances because the passionate expression of her feelings made me uncomfortable and convinced me it would not be safe to reveal my perspective on the issue if it was different than hers. I thought if I disagreed, she would vent all her passion and frustration on me.

A few times I did express my disagreement in an attempt to give Jan a different perspective, and it worked out just like I feared it would. Thus, I tried to appear to agree with her in an attempt to calm her emotions. I told myself I could sacrifice my perspective for hers. It was, I thought, a true expression of my love for her. As I write this, with more than twenty years of healing in this area, I see how blind and distorted my view of biblical love was. At the time, however, it seemed right and noble. But let me be clear: biblical love is sacrificial, but it is not enabling, nor is it motivated or controlled by fear, and it is certainly not dishonest!

When I first entered vocational ministry, Jan was right beside me, as she still is today, supporting, partnering, and serving with me every step of the way. She and I would regularly discuss issues being addressed as the church grew and developed. She often expressed opinions with passion and a clear perspective that pointed toward a specific direction. Sometimes I felt she expected immediate action from the perspective we were discussing in our conversation, and I felt pressured to act. This caused me to resist her and the pressure I felt.

It was fantastic when her perspective lined up with mine. However, difficulty arose when they didn't line up. Again, at first I would attempt to give her a different perspective on the issue of her concern or opinion. The pleasing side of me wanted to help her come to the point of agreement with what was being done in the church. I didn't realize the way I reacted and responded to her sharing was actually hurtful and invalidated her perspective. Feeling invalidated, she would attempt to help me understand her perspective, and I would respond in a further attempt to help her understand my more "excellent way." The fight was on!

After many heated discussions, I concluded it was better to remain silent, believing that would avoid hurting her or invalidating her through my responses. I listened as she passionately gave her perspective, interacting with "uh huhs" and some head nods as a reflection of my engagement in the conversation. Jan interpreted my acknowledgement of her sharing and lack of disagreement as reflective of me agreeing with her. In actuality it was my way of avoiding conflict.

In our conversations my passive response to Jan's passionate perspective gave her nothing to connect with. She could just as easily been interacting with one of our toddler children—it would have been about as satisfying to her as our conversation, and maybe more validating! Ultimately that passive-aggressive cycle of relating as a method of avoiding conflict erected a barrier of disconnection that we had to eventually tear down.

It felt like Jan knew no boundaries when it came to expressing her opinions. Although I might not agree with her, I kept my thoughts to myself to keep harmony between us. Yes, keeping my thoughts to myself cut down on the incidences of conflict, but it did not produce a truly open and honest relationship in our marriage.

I kept her off balance and confused and struggling to understand me by saying one thing and doing something entirely different. When I projected that knowing all the facts of a situation would make her mad, I gave her incomplete information about issues we were discussing. I didn't lie to her by telling her things I knew weren't true; I just presented information in a way that led her to erroneously conclude things, and I gave her little or no disagreement in order to avoid conflict. Inevitably the complete facts would somehow be revealed, and Jan would ask me to explain the incomplete information I had given her. In my explanation I tried to convince her that we had discussed the facts—which we had, but in shadowy, incomplete details. I suggested she must have forgotten the full details. I justified my method of relating— knowing the truth but not presenting *all* the truth in order to lead her to a false conclusion, which is actually lying and manipulation—by deciding it was better for our relationship if she didn't know all the facts. My passive way of relating took on a sinful expression, and it produced confusion for my wife. This is something I deeply regret and hope to help you avoid.

Often I allowed Jan to believe our perspectives were the same on an issue, that our feelings were the same, in order to avoid conflict. When they weren't the same, she usually had no clue because I gave her incomplete information or I kept silent, keeping her from knowing the real me. In order to avoid conflict and create harmony, I did not act or speak from the conviction of my heart unless there was no other option. Our relationship was shallow and unfulfilling, and neither of us understood why. I certainly did not connect my behavior with the problems we were encountering in our marriage.

I falsely believed that through my passive behavior I was managing my emotions in a healthy way, but nothing could be further from the truth. Since I did not express my feelings, they had no way of finding validation. Like a gas leak at a fitting in your furnace, my feelings behind the scenes were creating dangerous conditions, just waiting for a combustible moment. By stuffing my feelings over issues, I created a powder keg of destructive emotions that were waiting for the right event to ignite the fuse and bring about a relational explosion between us. At the most unexpected times, these emotions would erupt in what seemed to be an uncharacteristic angry or vindictive response. In reality the conditions for the explosion were created by my passive handling of circumstances.

Let's Talk About You

Has this chapter identified characteristics that you see in yourself? Is it time for things to change in your marriage?

In order to develop a healthy relationship style in your marriage, you must begin by acknowledging your behavior and its impact on your spouse and on your marriage. This will open the door that will enable you to identify and deal with the unhealthy thinking that may have created a stronghold in your life, causing dysfunction or disruption to your ability to develop the relationship you want and that God has planned for you and your wife.

Join with us in the next few chapters as we go deeper in our discussion to uncover the dynamics of passive-aggressive behavior. You will find personal healing and learn how to relate in healthy ways in your marriage so that you can openly and honestly know and love your wife, building the marriage relationship you desire.

When Jesus said, "You shall know the truth, and the truth shall set you free" (John 8:32, MEV), He meant the truth would set you free!

Chapter 2

BORN FREE

✧ JAN ✧

T HERE I WAS, LYING FLAT ON MY BACK IN THE hallway, looking up at the ceiling. What just happened? Tom had walked me to my high school English class, and we were standing outside the door talking before the bell rang. I could tell he wasn't really engaging in our conversation, and I asked him what he was going to do the next period. He said a bunch of the guys were going to play basketball in the gym and he was going to join them. He kept trying to bring our conversation to an end, and I could tell he was antsy to go, so I told him to go ahead and leave— he didn't have to stick around and talk to me. He said, "No, I want to talk to you!" But it was obvious he wanted to be somewhere else.

So after several of these interchanges I said, "Just go ahead and leave—I have to go to the bathroom." I walked away toward the bathroom in a huff, leaving Tom standing at the classroom door, holding his gym bag. He called to me to stop, but I turned up my nose and strutted down the hall.

The next thing I knew, I was flat on my back! He had thrown his gym bag like a bowling ball down the hallway at me, and it hit me at the back of my knees. It knocked my legs out from under me, and I fell back on top of his gym bag.

He ran up to me, all concerned, and asked, "Are you OK?" When I realized what had happened, I started laughing. I was laughing so hard, I could hardly talk. He started laughing too, but I told him not to take my laughing as an indication that what he had done was OK because he was in such big trouble. We both continued laughing while he helped me up and I gathered my composure. By now the bell had rung, signifying we were both late for class.

We had many of these types of situations where Tom would not honestly share what he was thinking, so I would react in a dramatic way in an attempt to get him to open up and share his true feelings with me. Our relational dynamic also had its fun-loving side where we really enjoyed each other, but this unhealthy element was a problem that would continue for years into our marriage. This element reflected strongholds of destructive thoughts that lay beneath the surface of our relationship and that, despite our love for each other, caused hurt, misunderstanding, and the need for healing.

OPPOSITES USUALLY ATTRACT— AND WE'RE NO EXCEPTION

Tom and I became friends in junior high as we sat next to each other in study hall. I actually still have notes from him somewhere in my memorabilia box in the attic! In fact, note-writing and talking to my friends in study hall are the reasons the study hall teacher and I did not get along. He thought you needed to be quiet and study in study hall. I completely disagreed with him and thought it was a perfect time to catch up with all my friends. Tom was that person who really thought study hall was a time for studying, and I regularly shocked him with my attitude toward our study hall teacher. It was my attitude coupled with a desire to have fun and not be bored that kept me in constant trouble in study hall. But I eventually figured out it was more fun studying than sitting in the corner facing the wall.

This dynamic of my being fun-loving and outrageous and Tom following all the rules and doing the right thing laid a foundation for misunderstandings and marital dysfunction between us that lasted for many years. The things that attracted us to each other were the things that ended up causing grief and pain in our relationship.

I will never forget the first time Tom asked me out. We were juniors in high school and had a typing class together. Tom sat in front of me, and one day he turned around, looked at me, and said, "Hey, do you want to go out Friday night?" I said, "Sure!" and then the teacher said, "Tom Lane, turn around and move your desk to the other side of the room." When the bell rang, he left the class—he didn't look at me or talk to me. He just disappeared. I wasn't sure if we had a date or not! He found me after school, we made plans for our first date, and our relationship began.

I was attracted to Tom's calm, steady personality and the way he could just sit and listen to conversations so nonjudgmentally—while I, on the other hand, was full of opinions. He was fun and easygoing. His ability to listen to me and not jump in with his opinion was so novel to me. I felt safe and accepted when I was with him. I felt like I could be myself and that he really "got me." I was the carefree, bold one who wasn't afraid to say or do anything. He was the one who followed rules and stayed calm in the middle of a crisis.

In my immaturity and naivety I really thought that on the inside Tom was just like me—but that he was putting on a front and acting like someone different on the outside. This thinking would be reinforced in me until he acted in a way that was not the way I would have acted. Then I felt the need to try to help him act in a more honest way—to be more real instead of holding back his true personality. He would listen to what I was saying and nod his head as I was talking, which I took as his agreement with me, so I was constantly surprised that his later actions didn't match up with his words to me. I stayed confused by our communication much of the time because he did not do what I thought he said he would do. Although confused, I never thought his inconsistent actions meant he didn't agree with me.

We dated through high school, and after we graduated, Tom was ready to get married. I was not ready to settle down yet, and there was constant friction between us over that issue. I thought we were way too young to make that decision, but he was ready to check that item off his "things to do after gradu-ation" list. *Get married—check.* So I went away to college for a year and had a great time meeting new people and visiting new places. The first semester I was gone, though, Tom pined away for me, and every time we talked he tried to make me feel guilty for having fun and leaving him. When he realized that wasn't working, he started dating around, and I was actu-ally happy for the pressure relief.

When I came home from that first year of college, Tom was ready to talk about getting married again. I was still in the college fun mode and still not ready to commit to marriage, so the pressure mounted quickly. We decided to talk to our pastor about our situation, and he gave us wise advice that solidified our future. He counseled us not to date each other for three months. The whole entire summer! We could say hi when we saw each other, but no phone calls, no group dates, and no hanging out. I was sad and yet relieved the pressure would be off. Tom was devastated. But we did it, and after a summer apart and lots of soul searching, I realized Tom was the person I wanted to spend the rest of my life with. I found a job, and we got married after Tom's sophomore year in college.

A Woman's Role . . .

The challenging thing about getting married so young is that you haven't had enough life experiences to teach you about other people and how to deal with them—especially the one you married! While we were preparing for marriage, we read all kinds of marriage books because we wanted to have a successful relationship. We were full of hope and excitement for our future. We felt like we had a good relationship and a good understanding of what marriage involved and how it should look. But after dating for four years we could not have been less prepared for marriage! The reality is that marriage is a lot of work, and the simple answers we read in those books often didn't apply to our situation.

When Tom and I were dating, I felt the freedom to be myself. We didn't have conversations about roles and rules. But as we began our marriage, we started looking for rules to help ensure we would have a successful marriage.

Then as we became involved in ministry, we began to hear teachings about a woman's role in marriage and what it was supposed to look like, which was great, but the woman described was nothing like me. I felt like things had been working OK in our marriage, but I slowly began to feel a pressure that I needed to be different, to look different, and to act different in order to be a godly wife. I loved God and felt if this was really what God was saying, then I would try do it because I wanted to please Him. I loved the leaders in our church and our pastor, and I never thought I was less than equal with them, but some of the teachings I was listening to and the things I was reading seemed to imply I was not as valuable as my husband. I thought I was being required to give up my thinking and my reasoning in order to honor Tom.

Thus began my journey into becoming what I thought a submissive wife should be. As time went on, I also began to lose my confidence in my voice, in my walk with the Lord, in my partnership with my husband, and in who I was as a woman. When decisions needed to be made, Tom was ready to make them, and it didn't seem to matter what I thought or felt. Occasionally I would think, "Why am I even here? What difference do I make? I don't have a voice, and my opinion is not valued."

By the way, just because Tom struggles with passivity doesn't mean he can't make decisions. When I stepped aside and rolled out the carpet for him to do so, he was more than able to walk on through. The problem is that it's not in my nature to roll out the carpet for someone else. I want to be involved and have a voice! That's where our two natures created conflict and struggle between us in our marriage.

Because I was trying to be a good wife, I began to squelch my feelings and ideas. I would share less and less what I was feeling and thinking. I was confident in my relationship with God and His love for me, but I was losing my confidence in this new role. I somehow picked up the idea that Tom's opinion was the one to be listened to and valued and that mine was not important. My role was to support him, run the house, take care of the kids, and let him be the head of everything. That was not actually possible because in reality I was home all day running the show and making decisions constantly. But I believed he was supposed to be in charge of decisions, so I felt guilty if I made decisions without asking him first. I was trying to do this marriage thing the "right" way, but I felt as if I was losing my voice in the process.

I remember the first time it was painfully obvious to me that what I wanted was not important. Tom and I had received a Sport Rally Nova as a wedding gift from my parents. It was fully loaded and beautiful! I loved that car, and it held sentimental value for me. I just assumed Tom loved our car too, but five years into our marriage Tom came home from work and told me he wanted to trade it in. I was surprised because I didn't know he was even thinking about it, but he said he needed something different for work. He had been looking at cars and had found one he liked. He wanted me to go with him to look at it.

I put it off for a few days, but Tom kept pressing the issue. Finally I went with him to the dealership. I assumed he was looking at a really cool car to replace our sporty Nova. But then he showed me the car he was considering, and I was totally underwhelmed. It was a plain white four-door Malibu with blue cloth seats—as blah as they come. I pointed out that the back windows didn't even roll down and it was so boring, but nothing I said mattered. It was as though I wasn't even there! Tom had decided he had to have this car, so he went inside to negotiate the deal and came out with the new car.

To say I was furious would be an understatement. I was devastated. We drove down to the dealership in a car I loved and came home with a car I hated. I cried so hard over that stupid car. This whole experience defined for me what I felt like my married life was becoming: a place where my opinions didn't matter, so why should I even give one? As an opinionated person, this was very painful.

Let me stop here and say that for some women, having a marriage in which the man is dominant and makes the decisions is a comfortable thing. They love the feeling of being taken care of and protected, and don't have a burning desire to input their ideas. They feel safe and stable and flourish in this environment. It is very fulfilling to them. But for other women, like me, this kind of arrangement is not comforting. It is stifling! I want to be involved in solving the problems in our lives. I want to be a helper. I need to collaborate and be heard. But though it didn't seem to feel right or fit at the time, I think we both bought into these roles of what a biblical marriage should look like.

Eventually, You'll Start Hobbling

Being in a marriage that doesn't fit is kind of like wearing a pair of shoes that don't fit; they may look good, but at the end of the day your feet hurt and you hobble around. Unlike a shoe that you can just throw out, a marriage is not disposable. As our marriage progressed and we were exposed to more teachings about what roles we were to have in marriage, it was as if we began wearing shoes that did not fit. We were trying to fit into molds that were not us. Looking back on it now, I realize you can wear a shoe that doesn't fit for only so long. At some point you have to take it off and admit, "This just isn't working."

For us, this happened when summer was drawing to a close one year. I remember I was twenty-eight and our third child was only a few months old. Tom and I had settled down for the night and things finally came to a head. We had turned off the lights and were lying in bed when Tom put his arms behind his head, gave a contented sigh, and said, "I don't think I've ever been happier in our marriage than I am right now."

I tried to respond, but I couldn't even get the words out of my mouth. I started shaking. I began to cry and just kept crying. I finally managed to say, "I cannot believe you just said that. I was lying here thinking that I have never been so miserable in all my life."

Tom was shocked because he thought our marriage was perfect. I was shocked that he could be so clueless. We began to talk about our different ideas of the roles of men and women in marriage. This event caused us to begin to take stock of our relationship and see where we were going off the track.

Looking back, I am surprised at how the teachings on submission during the early days of my marriage could have caused such havoc and confusion regarding my role and identity. It was like I was being handed a list of dos and don'ts and being told certain behaviors were more acceptable than others so I needed to shape up and get in line. I tried at first, but slowly I was shutting down—becoming less the vibrant Jan that I had been and more the quiet woman who had no voice.

It just wasn't working. This wasn't me, and I had no idea how to blend what I was learning with who I am.

As I tried to figure out why I was so unhappy, I began to realize I was not feeling valued or empowered to be the best me that I could be. I am an expressive, passionate, and opinionated person. I like to interact and exchange ideas. I like trying new things and hearing lots of different perspectives on ideas. I hate to be involved in anything that lacks purpose or leadership. In fact, if there is no leadership, I am quick to jump in and lead even if I don't know where we are going! I like to get to the bottom line and then ask questions to fill it all in later rather than hear all the details first and then the bottom line. I may come to conclusions before I hear all the facts, and I tend to think I'm right about what I'm saying—or else why would I be saying it? I freely share my opinions whether they are asked for or not.

This dynamic is a setup for trouble if you are clueless, like I was, to the effect it is having on the other person.

Tom and I were very committed to our marriage, and we wanted to do what was right; we just needed to find what was right for us. Without even realizing it, we were trying to find a formula for our marriage at the expense of developing our own relationship. There isn't a "one size fits all" guideline to having a perfect marriage. Every marriage is made up of two people with distinct personalities, backgrounds, strengths, and weakness; therefore, every single marriage is different. We found that marriage doesn't work according to a formula; it's a relationship between two very unique people.

As such, we shouldn't compare the way we live out our marriage relationship with the way someone else does it. This only leads to frustration and disappointment and even judgments. God wants us to have unity and peace in our marriage.

This happens when we embrace each other, differences and all, while finding our own identity in Christ.

Let's Talk About You

Have you ever thought you were a square peg trying to fit into a round hole? It's just not something that works. To all of you who have been told that you don't fit or you are not enough, let me tell you something: you are just who God made you to be. You are not a mistake or an accident. I want to help you figure out how you can live in a good relationship with your spouse, who is probably the total opposite of you. Let's learn how you can have a marriage full of unity, peace, strength, and companionship while becoming the person God made you to be.

Tom and I always said we had a good marriage, and we did. But we have learned that marriage is a journey, not a destination. If you have ever been on a long road trip, you know there are interruptions. Potty breaks, detours, car troubles, and arguments are all a part of the journey. We were experiencing that a good marriage can be messy and may not always look like it should, and that's because it is never finished—*we're* not finished. We are still on our journey, still learning things about each other, about communication, and about what works and doesn't work in our marriage. The same is true for you and your spouse.

I am so thankful Tom and I didn't give up on our marriage and didn't stay in a place of hurt and dysfunction. We worked individually and together to take responsibility for our behavior, and we partnered together to build a satisfying, healthy marriage relationship—and you can too. Let's continue forward to help you to build the marriage partnership that reflects God's unique work in you.

Chapter 3

THE THIEF THAT DESTROYS

❧ TOM ❧

WHEN I WALKED IN THE HOUSE FROM WORK THAT evening, Jan was at the stove preparing dinner. Our eyes made quick contact as I gave her a kiss and said, "Hey, babe!" and she responded back, "Hey," as I turned down the hall to our bedroom to change my clothes. As I headed out of the kitchen, the thought came to me: "She seems mad at me. Why is she mad at me? What have I done?" This internal dialog in my head continued: "I didn't call her—that's it. I know she likes me to call during the day. But I had a busy day. She needs to know that some days I just can't call. She needs to cut me some slack!"

This pattern of having inner conversations had become ingrained in my thinking and was always triggered when I sensed impending conflict or possible rejection. This particular inner dialog led me down the road of a negative interpretation of Jan's actions and possible reaction to me in our exchange. It had become such an ingrained response that I headed down that road without involving her in any part of the conversation. It took place all within myself.

It was this pattern of inner conversations that became the trigger for my passive-aggressive responses toward Jan. These inner dialogues acted as internal sirens that called me to battle stations. They stirred my instincts to circle the emotional wagons and brace for a conflict collision. In response to all that was going on in my mind, I would arm myself with the torpedoes of passive-aggressive responses—such as a sullen silence, withdrawal, or stubborn resistance—and I would prepare to fire those torpedoes below the surface of our relationship to defend against the threat of rejection I was feeling or the pending confrontation that appeared to be developing in our relationship.

As we discussed in chapter 1, passive-aggressive behavior is usually demonstrated in situations we feel are a direct threat to our emotional or physical well-being. It becomes a response to circumstances we determine are out of our ability to influence or control. It refers to the evasive, hidden tactics employed within a relationship that are intended to help us avoid or respond to circumstances of conflict or rejection.

In reality, though, these responses lead us to dishonest patterns of communication and behavior in the way we relate to others. The patterns are designed to appease on the surface but ultimately protect the internal emotions and position of the person executing them because of an expected collision. Passive-aggressive behavior in a marriage creates an invisible wall between a man and his wife that prevents the development of a real, open, and honest relationship between them.

When the passive-aggressive pattern of response is ingrained in a relationship, it becomes natural to the point of being an instinctive reaction in one or both of the partners. In my relationship with Jan it surfaced in a variety of circumstances—never announcing itself as passive-aggressive, of course—and embedded itself in the internal conversations I described above. With the internal sirens calling me to battle stations and the torpedoes of response loaded, I would wait for the right firing point. My relational "rules of engagement" would not let me fire unless fired upon, but I was loaded and ready if—when—I felt that happening.

A WORD ABOUT LABELS

Let me stop here and say that I hate putting labels on people, and I especially hate being labeled. I have spent most of my adult life trying to avoid wearing a label that someone else put on me. You may have similar feelings. If so, I would understand your hesitation to even begin investigating your method of interacting in your relationships, especially in your marriage.

So let me offer this perspective first. No cookie-cutter molds were used when God created you in the womb, and neither Jan nor I want to introduce a cookie-cutter response to the relational patterns of interaction in a marriage. God has created each person and every marriage unique. Even though every man has similar physical characteristics as other men, our similar characteristics do not take away the uniqueness of each one. We are men and we are unique, every one of us, in our personal makeup and expressions in life. This is equally true when it comes to our relational interactions.

I do not want to use a label to rob you of the individual uniqueness of who you are and how God created you! Jan and I recognize your uniqueness even as we identify characteristics and patterns of relating from our own experience. We present them as tools for you to use in your relationship as you work to establish and deepen the connection in your marriage. I have actually come to understand that the reason we label types of behavior and define characteristics associated with the different behavior types is not so the labels can be used against us or by us against our spouses. Rather, they help us understand ourselves and, out of that place of understanding, build healthy and satisfying marriages.

Believe Me, I Can Relate

Speaking for myself, I became aware of the strength of my resistance to labels and stereotypes a number of years ago when I was doing some reading on the subject of codependence. I was not looking to gain a greater understanding on the subject for the purpose of self-discovery (I was still resistant to that whole matter!) but rather to help other couples who were struggling in their marriages.

In studying codependent behavior, I came across a book by Pat Springle titled *Codependency*[1] and began reading a chapter each night before I went to bed. As I read, I found myself mentally engaging in agitated debate with the author in a growing resistance to the things he was saying in the book. As he presented a detailed discussion of the subject of codependency, I found myself responding defensively as though his book was a letter written to attack me. Each night as I read, I feverishly underlined phrases and made notes in the margins of the book. Rather than gaining insight related to the subject of codependency, I became more and more agitated.

Jan took notice of my growing negative responses with a certain degree of curiosity and concern. One night as she observed my fuming and fussing and listened to my angry dialog with the author, who obviously wasn't present, she said to me, "If reading that book bothers you so much, why don't you stop reading it?" To which I responded, "I think I will. He makes me so mad, if I met this guy face-to-face, I would punch him right in the nose!" It was obvious to Jan—but not so clear to me—that Pat Springle had touched a nerve in my life.

The strength of my reaction was based on what I perceived was the author's condescending attitude toward people's personal problems. I thought his descriptions created labels and stereotypes that devalued the individual uniqueness of each person's life. My reaction had nothing to do with the fact that his writing on the subject cast a long shadow on my personal behavior (or so I thought). It was his attitude; it was just wrong. He seemed rude, insensitive, and arrogant in his presentation of people's behavior, and someone needed to settle the injustice of it all on behalf of all mankind—or at least the part of mankind he was stereotyping with his labels! I told Jan I would welcome the opportunity to vent my frustration and settle the injustice Pat Springle created, if not for all mankind, then at least on behalf of everyone who had been impacted by his book and were as offended as me.

Jan, on the other hand, did not have the same reaction to labels or stereotypes that I did. To her, knowing characteristics of different personality types could be a useful tool to assist in her understanding of herself and others. She saw the description of codependency as a general characterization of behavioral traits, not as a personal attack. She found it helpful in understanding, building, and strengthening relationships. She was truly perplexed by my furious response.

I have come to agree with Jan regarding the helpfulness of labels. However, back then my response to her explanation of the benefit of labels was, "Whatever." I did not understand, nor could I relate to her interest in and affinity toward such things.

I thought she was wrong in her assessment of labels and the people who promote their use. How could labels be useful tools to benefit anything? I was convinced that with time and proper information, she would change her mind.

I now realize she was not wrong, but neither was I right. We both had legitimate perspectives. Labels and stereotypes can be used wrongly to hurt and limit others or they can be used as very helpful tools to further an understanding of yourself and others. Their impact depends on the motive of the person using them.

I allowed fear of label abuse to justify my resistance, and it clouded my ability to recognize my own destructive patterns of behavior and their impact on my relationship with Jan. It was my resistance and the resulting blindness that kept me from being able to acknowledge my passive-aggressive style of relating. My belief that I was a unique individual dealing with unique situations kept me from gaining any benefit from descriptions related to my behavior. I wanted no label put on me. I maintained that I didn't fit into any stereotype.

Is that how you feel? Let me assure you that I understand your concern and that I desire my identification of the characteristics associated with passive-aggressive responses to be used as a tool to benefit your relationship rather than as a weapon to defend your behavior or to highlight and criticize the ways you are different from your wife.

I have tried to illustrate with some of the stories of our relationship how passive-aggressive behavior reflects an unhealthy response to conflict as it harbors and catalogs a dishonest pattern of communicating. In my life it had its roots in a system of thinking that avoided direct confrontation (which is the passive part) but attempted to gain control of circumstances through subtle manipulative responses (which is the aggressive part). If you've ever thought about "teaching your wife a thing or two" or "making her pay a price" for something you've never directly discussed with her, you've stepped into the devious and sneaky world of passive-aggressive responses in your relationship.

There is no one specific behavior that can be described as passive-aggressive. It is not passive-aggressive to think before you respond to a circumstance—the Bible calls that wisdom (James 1:19). Also, you are not passive-aggressive if you draw boundaries in your relationship in response to an unhealthy behavior or reaction from your spouse. As I said earlier, passive-aggressive responses are the result of unhealthy thinking that influences our behavior, and they manifest in a variety of ways in our relational interaction.

What It Can Look Like

Passive-aggressive responses are connected with uncommunicated expectations in the relationship. Here is an example of how it surfaced in our marriage. I might come home from work and help Jan with the kids or lend my assistance with chores around the house. Say I remove the dishes from the table after dinner and load them in the dishwasher, telling Jan to go sit in the family room and relax, insisting that she step away from me and the kids to enjoy some alone time by watching TV or reading a book. This might come from a sincere desire on my part to help my wife and to bless her with a little break—there's nothing wrong with serving and ministering to your wife. But in my case it also carried a subtle, uncommunicated expectation that Jan would do something nice for me in return. No specific action was associated with the expectation, nor did I have a time frame in mind for her to reciprocate. It was just an unspoken expectation that a reciprocating action would come from her to serve me back somehow.

My expectation was uncommunicated and subtle, but it carried with it the thought that my payback time was coming. This expectation brought with it a hidden ledger in my mind where I kept track of the nice things I had done. I logged them as something owed, like a debt to be repaid to me at some point by Jan. This was so subtle that I was blind to it. Jan was unaware of it as well, since I had not openly communicated it, but she felt the pressure. In fact, she would look at me at times and say, "I feel like you want me to perform for you." I denied that statement with shock and offense, but under the surface my inner dialog was keeping tabs.

What's more, the longer an act of kind service went unreciprocated, the more my internal dialog would take on the role of debt collector and remind me that the expected return on my acts of service had not been paid. It would remind me reciprocation was overdue. My inner conversation would convince me that if my act of service to Jan was going to be repaid with a reciprocal act of kindness on her part, I was going to have to make it happen or remind her it was owed.

I was overly aware of the nice things I did for Jan and monitored them like a credit manager watches the accounts of his customers. At different times I would think to myself, "This would be the perfect time for Jan to reciprocate with an act of service"—kind of like a return on my investment. I might even help her out with a subtle hint—nothing direct and nothing open or completely honest. If she failed to pick up on the hint, it hurt my feelings, as it led me to conclude her lack of response was a willful decision of rejection aimed at me. When I interpreted her lack of action in this way, it called for further passive-aggressive behavior from me in defensive retaliation. This uncommunicated conclusion on my part was fueled by the internal debt collector dialog going on in my head that increased its volume and urgency with each unreciprocated act. My feelings of rejection triggered the arming of my passive-aggressive torpedoes. Concluding Jan's behavior was obviously an act of war that called for a response, I prepared my attack.

All this took place without Jan's knowledge, since I was not openly communicating my thoughts and expectations to her. Even though I had not communicated my expectations or my desires, I concluded her lack of action was her willful rejection of me. It translated as a reflection of her diminished love toward me. It led me to conclude she didn't love me as much as I loved her. In my hurt and rejection I would withdraw into my inner dialog and stew over her inaction. My anger would grow. Out of my frustration, related to that hidden, never-discussed desire or expectation, I would fire the torpedoes of passive-aggressive responses—usually sullenness, withdrawal, and stubborn resistance—using them to get Jan's attention and ultimately creating a confrontation between us.

Rarely did I get the response I wanted. My act of war was a provocation that usually escalated the confrontation into an outright fight. Jan fought with me on the surface while I fought with her with guerilla-style tactics. She wanted an open, honest dialog and would aggressively confront things she felt were not right—no torpedoes under the surface from her and no sneaky punches below the emotional belt. That was my response to our conflict.

Jan would respond to my torpedoes by confronting the withdrawal and rejection she felt from me. She was direct, honest, and open in her communication, while I was subtle and communicating below the surface in relational Morse code. My communication was encrypted and required her to break the code if she was really interested in what was going on with me, if she really wanted to know what I was thinking or how I felt.

My passive-aggressive response was payback—a retaliatory attack—to teach her a lesson, raise her awareness, and increase her sensitivity. When I fired my torpedoes, it did not usually happen in immediate response to a singular event but rather as a reaction against an accumulated frustration that had built up in my mind from a series of uncommunicated and unreciprocated actions that had created expectations. I was awaiting reciprocation for the accumulated total of my acts of kindness and service.

I could be very benevolent and understanding with my responses if I saw a good-faith effort on Jan's part to respond to me in just the right way. But when I concluded her behavior was ignoring me and unappreciative of my sacrificial responses on her behalf, my internal dialog would call me to action like Dog the Bounty Hunter going after someone who had skipped their bail. I became mean and punitive in my subtle way as I sought to force a response from Jan. I would catch her at a time when she least expected it, hours or days removed from the situation over which I had been stewing, and I would launch my attack.

This method of addressing my frustrations confused her, hurt her, and pushed her away from me rather than drawing her closer. She became painfully aware I was mad, but she didn't know or understand why—and when she asked why I was mad, I would give her a false reason or deny I was angry at all. I felt if she had to ask why I was mad, she wasn't ready for a response.

Due to my dishonesty, Jan never really understood that my anger was a result of the rejection I felt, and neither did I. This rejection was something she never intended, brought on by my internal dialog over something she was not even aware had taken place. This pattern of relating repeated itself, like the seasons during a calendar year, throughout circumstances that arose from time to time in our family life—until with God's help, we identified the pattern and took steps to make it stop.

How I Broke Free

As I write this, I feel compelled to tell you how destructive and unhealthy my passive-aggressive responses were to our relationship. I am amazed that I thought of myself as emotionally healthy and "in the right" in these responses. I am so thankful God intervened and that through Jan's commitment to God and her love and commitment to me, she hung with me long enough to see me come to an awareness of my unhealthiness and worked with me to break free from that way of thinking. I am thankful we now enjoy a satisfying relationship that is based on open, honest communication. I now recognize and appreciate the sacrificial expressions of love she has always demonstrated to me but that my internal dialog and torpedoes of passive-aggressive behavior blinded me from seeing and receiving.

The breakthrough actually began with my resistance to the concepts in Pat Springle's book. While I struggled to receive from him the concepts detailed in his book, I found another book on the topic of codependency by Margaret Rinck. I began reading her book *Can Christians Love Too Much?*[2] Dr. Rinck presents similar concepts in her book but in a way that was easier for me to swallow. As I gained an understanding of the issues, I began to realize what I was doing to undermine our relationship. With Jan's help, we worked together to identify the unhealthy pattern of thinking that formed this stronghold of response in my life.

The breakthrough came like sun does when it breaks through cloud cover on an overcast day. When the sun shines through, you can suddenly see things with greater clarity. The sun broke through on that day I walked into the house and greeted Jan while she was standing at the stove, cooking dinner—the story that began this chapter—and as it did, it provided clarity and understanding about my passive-aggressive responses. That convergent point happened as I turned down the hallway toward the bedroom on my way to change my clothes. I was at the corner of the familiar road of negative interpretation in my inner dialog. It was a road I knew well by this time. I also knew it was a road that led to passive-aggressive responses and more barriers in our relationship—barriers we were working hard to dismantle. I heard the hurt and rejection in my internal dialog calling me down that road. I recognized the road signs and reminded myself I did not want to travel down that road. I knew its destructive results.

As I was standing at the corner to that road in my mind, deciding whether to turn down that path or not, Jan came into the bedroom where I was changing and asked in a bubbly voice, "So, how was your day?" I was at the moment of decision, and her voice was the voice of health and healing calling me to a deeper relationship and connection with her, and it encouraged me to make the right choice.

But a decision to not go down that road was not enough. The decision had to be followed by action for healing to take effect and the barrier to be lowered. All my emotions were screaming at me to take a defensive position. I was caught between these two voices in internal debate as I was evaluating her response and contemplating my reaction. My inner voice beckoned me to interpret her question through my own familiar filters of passive-aggressive behavior and negative interpretation. Numerous times I had unleashed a passive-aggressive torpedo into our relationship while denying to her face the very attack I was unleashing. Now my inner thoughts were telling me not to trust her, to believe she was doing the same to me. It accused her of covering her impending attack with a cheery voice that would soon turn into an attack on me.

To stop the inner dialog, I had to take a stand and recognize the sick process seeking to reinsert itself into my thinking and control my actions. I had to make a decision to refuse to listen to that familiar dialog. I had to override the passive-aggressive defense sirens going off in my head and make a different response.

So here's what I did.

I looked at Jan and asked, "Are you mad at me?"

She immediately responded in her perky voice, "No."

With seriousness that seemed to her to be an overreaction and unnecessary based on our interaction in that situation, I said, "I need you to be completely honest with me, and if you are mad, I need you to tell me because everything in me is telling me to brace myself for rejection, conflict, or both. So if you tell me you're not mad but you really are mad, and your anger surfaces later, it is going to really mess me up."

Jan asked what I meant, why I was asking if she was mad. So I explained the inner dialog that was calling me to action—how I had perceived her response to me when I came into the house. I told her I recognized my internal dialog as part of the pattern we were working to break and that I needed her help to respond correctly in this instance. This level of honesty in our communication was new for me, but it was what we both wanted in our relationship.

She said to me, "Look into my eyes." So I looked into her eyes and she said, "I am not mad at you!"

I could tell by the look in her eyes, as she made that statement to me, that she was not mad. She was telling me the truth. So I overrode the passive-aggressive defense sirens going off inside me and openly, honestly told her about my day.

This honest dialog between us and the interaction it produced marked a turning point in our relationship and was a measurement of God's healing work to deliver me from the passive-aggressive responses that were instinctive to me. It broke the pattern of responses to the seasonal cycle of circumstances that marked our relationship and had created a barrier against connection that had caused hurt and stunted our developing heart-to-heart intimacy.

You're Not Alone

I'm not the only one who has had to learn this, and neither are you. I've counseled many couples through this same dynamic over the years. They, like Jan and me, needed to identify their unhealthy patterns of communication and then make choices to override their natural instincts to find true health and happiness.

Let's take one example. When Ben and Angie (not their real names) came to me, Ben was fully convinced their problems were totally because of Angie's aggressiveness. He ran a growing business and had several employees working with him. He had no problem managing his business or giving direction and oversight to his employees. His employees and customers loved his kindness and customer-service attitude. The success of the business provided a comfortable standard of living for his family. By all outward measures he was a success. He did all he could to provide his wife and children with much of what they wanted in life.

The frustration Ben and Angie felt was the result of their response to each other's behavior. Angie was resentful that Ben's customers and employees got more of his time and energy than she and the kids did. She had a laundry list of broken promises Ben had made, and she aggressively confronted him with her frustrations. The more broken promises piled up, the angrier Angie got—and the more expressive and intolerant she became with his behavior. On a couple of occasions she even went to his business and ranted and raved in front of employees and customers in an effort to get him to change, but nothing seemed to work.

Angie's constant whining, increasingly vocal demands, and growing aggression frustrated Ben. In order to avoid conflict between them, he would verbally agree to almost any demand she made, even if he knew he could not fulfill it. He felt there was no way to meet all her demands, but he did not communicate his true feelings because he felt she wouldn't understand or listen to what he felt but would only become more aggressive. Past efforts to communicate his feelings had only escalated the conflict between them.

What he wanted was peace. He silently and subtly resisted her aggressive demands while on the surface indicating his agreement in order to keep the peace. When he was trapped by Angie's aggression, Ben would become angry and his communication became harsh and curt, causing hurt and furthering the disconnection in their relationship. His attempt to avoid conflict with his wife had failed to create the peace he desired. He became defensive and developed a victim mentality, feeling sorry for himself. Angie's desperate, aggressive attempts to get her husband's attention and lead him to prioritize her and the kids only made matters worse. Initially he withdrew to avoid conflict, but when that didn't work, his anger surfaced and he went on the offensive, becoming mean, punitive, and retaliatory as he lashed out in response to her aggression.

Ben's behavior not only hurt Angie, it also totally confused her, leaving her unsure how to relate to Ben. He seemed like Dr. Jekyll and Mr. Hyde in the way he related to her. The problem between them went unresolved as Angie's aggression provoked responses of passive-aggression in Ben. In the process they were driven further apart as this pattern cycled in their relationship. They were discouraged, frustrated, and unfulfilled in their marriage. Thankfully through counseling we were able to identify the unhealthy pattern and show them a better way to relate and connect in their marriage.

Which Road Will You Choose?

In marriage counseling I have found that couples respond to the difficulties present in their relationships in one of three ways. Some determine that the problems are too great or too difficult, and they decide to cut their losses and start over in a new relationship. They file for divorce. Typically they repeat the pattern of dysfunction in a new relationship since they have not dealt with their unhealthy thinking.

Others don't want to start over, feeling that divorce is not an option, but they have lost hope anything will ever change. They develop coping mechanisms to deal with the dysfunction in their relationship. They remain together, but their marriage stops growing. It never changes, and they live life unfulfilled and frustrated in their marriage.

The third group acknowledges their frustration, confronts their problems honestly, and takes responsibility for their behavior. They address the issues by making personal changes, and as a result the barriers to happiness and fulfillment in their marriage are dismantled piece by piece, producing the relationship they have desired through their commitment and hard work.

For a long time I chose the second option. Jan and I were firmly committed to our marriage, but I sought to gain Jan's love and affection through unhealthy and dishonest communication. I didn't recognize it then, but my inner dialog and hidden responses created a false relationship based on things that were not real. My reactions to Jan's perceived motives were based on lies developed through internal conversations that made me feel hurt and rejected. My responses were subtle, mostly underground, and usually surfaced in an ambush or surprise attack. I related to Jan this way for many years in our marriage. I kept her off balance and confused. I created a barrier that prevented our marriage from becoming as satisfying and deep as we both desired.

If this unhealthy and destructive way of relating is reflected in your marriage, it is possible to change. If you are seeking to have your needs met or to express your anger and frustration by launching torpedoes of passive-aggressive responses, there is a better way that will lead you into a healthy, real relationship with your wife. I mistakenly thought my behavior stemmed from an honest effort to connect my heart with Jan's and share our life together, but the result was hurt, withdrawal, and frustration.

This is the kind of damage that is produced by passive-aggressive responses to circumstances of conflict in our marriages. But there is hope. You can reverse the damage and change the unhappiness in your marriage by changing the way you relate. You do not have to continue in this destructive, unhealthy cycle.

LET'S TALK ABOUT YOU

Every marriage has conflict. The question is, "What is the best, healthiest way to resolve conflict in your relationship?" We will discuss conflict resolution in a later chapter, so for now let me say that if you are trying to pacify the aggressive personality of your wife by telling her what you think she wants to hear, you are not avoiding conflict. You are at best delaying it. You cannot avoid conflict by moving it underground. In doing so, you lay the framework for a shallow, dishonest relationship that will not satisfy you or her. It is damaging to the relationship.

If you are a passive-aggressive man, you must take responsibility for changing the way you relate to your wife. Stop blaming her and take a look at yourself. Contrary to what the term *passive* may imply, men who relate through passive-aggressive behavior may have strong people skills and, because of these skills, can be highly successful in their careers. They can excel in team activities, whether at work or in athletics. They tend to be extremely sensitive and gentle toward others. Their sensitivity leads them to be giving and service-oriented in the way they relate to people. These qualities endear them to people they are around. On the surface they appear almost perfect, but those closest to them experience frustration, confusion, and hurt from their sneaky behavior.

To understand passive-aggressive behavior and be able to identify its effect on your relationship with your wife, you must first understand what it is. You must not run away from identifying it but rather must openly expose it in your life. Once it is exposed, you will be able to choose to override what has become natural in the way you relate as you work to build new patterns of relating in your marriage.

Without taking these simple action steps, the finger will always be pointed at the behavior of your aggressive wife and you will remain blind to destructive patterns of your responses. Make the choices needed to have a healthy relationship today, right now!

Chapter 4

THE STRONG WOMAN

✴ JAN ✴

F MERELY TALKING ABOUT OUR MARRIAGE COULD have made it better, then Tom and I would have built a good, strong marriage in two years. We were always talking about our relationship because it was important to us, and we wanted our marriage to be strong, healthy, and satisfying to both of us. But talking about our relationship did not get us where we wanted to go, and we didn't have the understanding or the tools we needed to handle the conflicts in our marriage. We strongly desired a great marriage, but we struggled to figure out how to get there.

I tried to be up front and honest with Tom in our communication, but as I related things to him, I usually didn't receive a satisfying response. The more passionate I was, the quieter he became. I tried to draw things out of him by asking direct questions. He would give short, compliant answers. When I tried to dig deeper, he would become quieter and less responsive. I would begin to feel hurt and rejected and press in harder, and then out of the blue he would get angry about something we weren't even talking about. I would feel off balanced in the conversation as I tried to respond to the random issue he raised, and it seemed like we never would resolve the real issues.

Whenever we argued, it felt as if Tom was holding things back from me, but he would vehemently deny it. I often told him our communication felt as if we were playing a game in which he knew the rules but wouldn't tell me what they were. I was left to figure it out on my own. I had to guess and try to figure out ways to connect with him. It felt unfair, and I was frustrated because I was doing my best to connect without ever being successful. There seemed to be nothing I could say or do to make him share with me.

I look back and realize that my efforts to connect with Tom through direct, passionate communication were the very things that caused him to shut down. Not being sensitive to relational nuances, I never really noticed when he began to withdraw. It was usually well into the conversation before I realized he wasn't responding with more than "Uh huh" or just smiling and nodding his head. When I did finally notice he wasn't engaging, this began a cycle of my pressing in more intently and demanding a response and his withholding and withdrawing. It produced very negative results.

We decided early in our marriage that no matter how much we disagreed on an issue or what else might be going on, we were committed to one another for the rest of our lives. We likened our marriage to a football game in the sense that we were both on the same team going for the same goal. We might be playing different positions, but no matter how different we saw things, we were still on the same team going for the same goal. We would remind each other of this when we were having a disagreement. One of us would stop and say, "You know, we are on the same team." This helped put things in perspective in the heat of an argument. It was a positive point of connection that would stop the face-off and bring our attitudes together again.

As we began to be established in ministry, we began counseling other couples about marriage problems, and this caused issues to surface in our own imperfect marriage. I would hear Tom giving advice I didn't agree with, and I would tell him about it. He would tell me what he was thinking, and I would tell him what I was thinking. Maybe I would tell him I thought what he had counseled was wrong. He would become defensive and respond with the reason he was right and I was wrong, and we would start this circular routine of arguing. Tom would say something like, "You always think you're right" or "You always have to win." I argued that I didn't want to win at all. I just wanted to be able to talk about things and come to an agreement. It confused me that he put it into a win/lose context because I thought we were trying to communicate. Tom would stand firm in his belief that I was competing with him and trying to win. Usually he went away from these conversations feeling hurt and defeated, and I went away feeling misunderstood and rejected. Neither of us received what we needed from these discussions.

You Don't Know What You Don't Know

Tom entered vocational ministry on his thirtieth birthday. He started out in the business department at the church and after a couple of years he became a pastor. He began overseeing the pastoral counseling ministry at our church, and they had started doing training on codependency, which interested me. I decided to read one of the books they were using.

It was titled *Codependency: Breaking Free From the Hurt and Manipulation of Dysfunctional Relationships* by Pat Springle.

I thought it was a great book, and I asked Tom if he had read it. He said no but that he wanted to read it so he could understand the issue of codependency. I told him he should read it because there were some things in there that I thought applied to our relationship.

He started reading the book at night, but it did not shed any light on our relationship for him. In fact, he did not like the book at all. He would become agitated and start writing in the margins and cross out sentences and complain that he did not agree with the ideas. It made him angry. I finally said, "Hey, if you don't like the book and don't agree with it, stop reading it." So he decided to stop.

A few weeks later he got ahold of another book called *Can Christians Love Too Much?* by Margaret Rinck. I read it too and thought it basically said the same things the other book had said. But something about the style of Dr. Rinck's writing caught Tom's attention, and he read it easily and agreeably. He was able to gather a lot of tools from that book for use in counseling and in our relationship.

One thing Tom said he realized about our relationship from that book was that he made assumptions about what I was feeling and thinking based on his own feelings and thinking. This caused many misunderstandings and confusion between us because we are nothing alike. We talked about this, and he said he wanted to change that dynamic in our communication. The opportunity presented itself a few days later. He came home from work while I was cooking dinner at the stove. He stopped and said hi, and I said, "Hey." Then he walked back to our bedroom to change his clothes. After I finished cooking,

I walked back to talk with him. I asked him how his day went and he said, "Good." Then he just stared at me.

I asked, "Is anything wrong?"

He said, "OK, I want to ask you something, and I want you to be honest with me. It is very important that you be totally honest with me."

I couldn't wait to hear what he was going to ask.

He asked, "Are you mad at me?"

I looked at him incredulously. We hadn't even spoken more than a few words, and I couldn't figure out what in the world he was talking about. I said, "No, I am not mad at you."

Tom replied, "Do you mean it? Because everything in me is telling me that you are mad at me."

I said, "Tom, look me in the eyes. I am not mad at you at all. Not in any way at all."

He asked again, "Are you sure?"

I said, "Tom, I promise I'm not mad at you at all, but I *will* get mad at you if you keep on asking me this!"

I watched him as he let it sink in that I wasn't mad. He visibly changed in front of me. It was like a light came on and he was relieved of a heavy burden.

This was a huge breakthrough in our marriage. He was choosing to trust what I was telling him above what his feelings were telling him. Although he had been tempted to withdraw from me, after this exchange he was able to change his attitude and engage with me as if there was nothing wrong. Because we were able to talk it through without getting frustrated or angry, we were able to hear each other and respond in a way that diffused the situation.

Much later I later figured out that the reason Tom didn't trust me when I said I wasn't mad at him was because if the tables were turned and he was the one being asked if he was mad, he would have said he was not mad—even if he was seething inside. He would have expected me to know he was mad even though he said he wasn't. Because he projected his feelings on me, he had to struggle to overcome the belief that I was mad at him. It was a scary and hard thing for him to go against those real feelings and to believe what I was saying, but it made a huge difference in our relationship.

My Part in the Equation

It took me many years to figure out that Tom had a hard time being honest about these kinds of feelings when I pressed him through direct confrontation. I didn't understand that the directness of my confrontation made him feel uncomfortable. He had a deep fear that if he shared how he really felt, I would reject him. He couldn't share honestly with me because of his fear of rejection, but his lack of honesty caused me to feel rejected too. We were both feeling rejected by each other in different ways.

As Tom had his internal dialog going on all the time, I had one too. I knew Tom had frustrations and resentments toward me, but I couldn't get him to admit it or to tell me what they were. Finally, when I had exhausted all my resources to get him to talk, I would just give up and move on and not wait for him to "come clean." I felt like if he was going to be dishonest, then I was justified in ignoring his hurt demeanor. I was always frank and honest in my interactions with him, and I expected him to figure out how to be open and honest with me. I was not sensitive or gentle in my reactions or responses because I was completely annoyed that he would not be honest with me. This kind of insensitivity on my part set us up for many hurtful conversations. I stood my moral high ground for truth at the expense of learning a new way of being sensitive to his need for peace.

When we talk to couples in seminars or classes, we often get questions afterward about how this dynamic between assertive women who are married to passive-aggressive men can work. The women talk about how confused and frustrated they are in trying get their husbands to open up to them, and I feel their pain. It is very hard to have a conversation with someone who will not engage. It is even harder to see and understand that you are a part of the problem—that you are doing things that have created this unhealthy dynamic. I call this the *aggressive-dominant versus passive-aggressive* style of communication.

The word *dominate* carries many negative connotations. By definition it means "to rule, exercise control, or to occupy a commanding or elevated position over a person or situation." Dominance can refer to the response a person asserts over another in a relationship. It can also refer to a personality that is aggressive and controlling, with those characteristics influencing the relational dynamics between the two people.

Maybe it would be true to say that both men and women resist being labeled as dominant. However, it seems as if a man who is labeled as dominant is seen through different eyes than a woman who is described as dominant. For the man it can even be a complimentary characteristic, showing strength and decisiveness. But for a woman it is never complimentary. It is always used as a derogatory statement and considered critical, negative, and unflattering. Many of the characteristics that define a successful woman—discipline, intelligence, drive, and ambition—are often the very traits that get her labeled as a dominant woman. The term is especially unflattering to a woman who wants to reflect godly characteristics. It goes against the scripture that says a woman's inner beauty is reflected in a gentle and quiet spirit (1 Pet. 3:4). How do the qualities of gentleness and quietness relate to a woman whose strength of personality is naturally expressed in ways that get her labeled as dominant?

When a woman is described as dominant or aggressive in a relationship, it usually means that through her manner of interacting in the relationship, she seeks to impose her will on individuals and circumstances, thus controlling the outcome. I couldn't see that my style of relating was aggressive or dominant. I knew in my heart that I was flexible and adaptable, but when it came to confrontation I had a "take no prisoners" approach. I wanted what I said to be heard, agreed with, and ultimately acted on. And since Tom didn't seem to care enough to put up a decent argument, I became a bully in many conversations, wanting things done my way or there could be arguing for hours.

Tom often said trying to get me to agree to something different than what I thought was like wrestling with an alligator. He felt like he had to wrestle me to the ground and pin me down to get me to change my mind—and he was not willing to do that. After a few rounds of arguing, he would back down, which led me to believe that he (finally) agreed with me. I couldn't see that he felt as strongly as I did but just wasn't willing to stay engaged in the debate. Since he became compliant during the discussion, I could bring the end of the conversation to my desired result. Then when a decision was made, I felt it represented both of us.

Consequently, I felt very betrayed when Tom did not act upon the things I thought we had agreed on. I would accuse him of lying to me because he would not tell me he didn't agree with me or that he wasn't going to do what I thought we had agreed on. He would instead tell me what he thought I wanted to hear so he wouldn't have to contend with me. I didn't realize his goal was to smooth over our conflict and bring it to a peaceful resolution in any way he could, which was more important to him than risking open, truthful communication that might further escalate the disagreement.

The degree of a dominating style of communication is represented on a scale that goes from assertive (harmlessly benign with good results) to destructively controlling (with negative results). In the most harmless way of being dominant in a relationship, a woman is able to compel the other person to agree with her using her intelligence and persuasive manner. In her most destructive and controlling expression of dominance, she asserts her perspective and demands or manipulates the other person to her desired result and makes sure they know it is going to be her way or the highway. She gets angry when things don't go her way and may take her anger out on those around her by yelling or becoming punitive. She also may become silent and stop talking to the offender. I call this the "freeze out." Either way there will be a price to pay for disagreeing with her.

Dominant people believe their way is the best way and will force it on the people around them even if it violates the others' convictions. Dominant individuals may be blind to the damaging effect this is having on their spouse and their relationship. In the process they may even become condescending and sarcastic toward their spouse if the spouse tries to disagree with them. This causes the spouse to feel violated, and he or she may feel rejected, intimidated, or furious.

Either way, it does not foster a warm, fuzzy feeling of love and mutual satisfaction in the relationship.

In our relationship Tom and I did not understand these dynamics. He didn't know his style of relating was passive, and I didn't see that I was aggressive. We just knew we were not able to relate to each other effectively or satisfactorily. We had a long way to go.

Let's Talk About You

Have you noticed that your husband avoids having difficult conversations with you? Maybe like me you recognize that you have some controlling and dominating tendencies in your style of relating. If you are seeing that your words and actions are having a negative effect on your marriage, you can do something about it. Remember that your relationship with your husband is more important than being "right" or getting your way.

Even if your husband seems like he doesn't mind giving up his desires and perspective to accommodate yours, you are undermining the opportunity to have a mutually satisfying relationship by not stopping and inviting him into the conversation. He is not willing to risk upsetting you by disagreeing with you unless he feels like he is respected and will be heard. This is a delicate dance that takes practice, patience, and maybe lots of hard work.

I want to encourage you that addressing the issues of a dominant style of relating will not require you to completely deny your strength of perspective and the gifts God has given to you. It does mean that you will have to take a closer look at what impact you are having on the relationships around you, especially with your husband. I encourage you to prayerfully consider what God might be saying to you and allow Him to shape your aggressive style of communication with clearer understanding so that you can connect more deeply and intimately with your husband.

Change is a process. Tom and I are still a work in progress, but we have a satisfying marriage and are so thankful we didn't give up when times got tough. You too can find satisfaction, joy, and fulfillment for your marriage. Don't give up!

Chapter 5

WHO'S YOUR DADDY?

❧ TOM ❧

I WAS EIGHT YEARS OLD AND WAS ACCOMPANYING my mom on her weekly trip to the grocery store. We were loading the shopping cart with the food items that a growing family of five required, along with a few extra items that my sisters and I talked our mom into buying. As we strolled down the drink aisle, we stopped to put a six-pack of RC Colas into the cart. As my mom placed the cokes in the cart, she pointed out to my sisters and me that each of us were entitled to two colas from the carton. They were ours to manage and consume in the next week, but when they were gone, that was it until the following week's shopping trip. She said in her best teaching voice, "You kids manage your drinks well," to which I thought, "Yeah, yeah, cool—we have some colas in the basket. That's good!"

A few days later it was family game night. It was time to pop popcorn, drink RC Cola, and have fun as a family. That night I drank both of my colas, despite a reminder from my mom that I was drinking my allotment for the week. In my view the moment demanded the full consumption of the available colas! A few days later my sisters were enjoying their second bottle of cola as they watched TV. I wanted to join them, but I had none left—my colas were gone. I told my mom we needed to go to the store to buy more RC Colas, at which point she reminded me I didn't manage my allotment as well as my sisters had, which was why they still had more to drink. She reflected back to our family game night and reminded me that I had consumed all mine while my sisters saved theirs to enjoy later.

This made me mad. I said in frustration to my mom, "When I grow up, I am going to have a soda machine in my living room, and I am going to remove the coin slot from the machine so my kids can have a soda any time they want!" I was unaware of the power of this vow and its possible effect on my life. It lay dormant through my developmental years at home. However, it did plant something in the psyche of my emotions. Buried in my heart, it quietly rested, waiting for the right time to unleash its influence. I was unaware of its presence and impact on me and my behavior until many years later.

It popped up when Jan and I were in our second year of marriage. It was the weekend, and we had some friends over to eat pizza and play games. We had been to the store to buy a six-pack of Pepsi to serve to our friends as we played games that evening. At the end of the night as we were cleaning up, I noticed all the Pepsis had been consumed while we were playing games. I pointed out to Jan that we were out of Pepsi and told her we needed to go to the store tomorrow to refresh our supply. She said matter-of-factly, "Oh, it can wait until I go to the store in a few days." When she said that, I erupted with a reaction that was much stronger than her response deserved. I told her we would never be out of sodas in our house—ever! I told her that she could either go to the store tonight or first thing tomorrow to refresh our supply, or I would go. We would not be out of Pepsi.

Jan stood back, shocked by the strength of my response. It even shocked me in the strength I expressed it, although it was reflective of the way I truly felt. In her sweet way she told me that I was being ridiculous but that she would get the Pepsi tomorrow. I didn't immediately link my response to the situation from my childhood. I didn't know why I felt so strongly. All I knew was that was the way I felt. I thought I was establishing a value of anticipating and meeting needs for my home and family.

It Goes Way Back

The impact of circumstances we have encountered through our lives come together in powerful ways to influence our behavior with lasting impressions many years later. God says it through Moses in the Ten Commandments this way: "I am God,your God, and I'm a most jealous God, punishing the children for any sins their parents pass on to them to the third, and yes, even to the fourth generation of those who hate me. But I'm unswervingly loyal to the thousands who love me and keep my commandments" (Exod. 20:5–6, The Message).

An iniquity or sin is simply a tendency or a bent toward a particular negative behavior. We know from research studies that many behavior traits are passed generationally. Alcoholism or addictive tendencies flow through family lines. Physical conditions such as high blood pressure, heart disease, cancer, and other physical ailments follow family lines. Physical, emotional, and verbal abuse follow family lines, along with a whole host of other personal, physical, and behavioral characteristics.

Even our observations confirm this spiritual truth. Have you ever observed your child responding in a way you didn't necessarily like and said to your spouse, "That response was just like…," and then associated it with a grandparent, aunt or uncle, or even yourself or your spouse? You are simply recognizing the impact on yourself and your family of the truth expressed by God.

It's kind of like that saying, "Who's your daddy?" Have you ever heard that before? This short phrase is much bigger and deeper than its three words imply. It could be rephrased to ask, "Who is influencing and shaping your life?" Or it could be made into multiple questions that ask, "Who has taught you your values, helped you discover your purpose, or given direction to your life?" The point is this: whatever or whoever is influencing you, shaping you, teaching you values, defining your purpose, or giving direction to your life, that's who your daddy is.

There is a difference between a father and a daddy. A father brings us into this world, but a daddy shapes and influences our lives as we move through it in circumstances and experiences. God intended our biological fathers to be daddies, but the truth is that not every father fills the role of a daddy—and even the best earthly daddies aren't perfect.

The reality is, someone or something is filling the role of daddy in the circumstances of your life. Without strategic guidance, the powerful spiritual influences of sin and iniquities impacting your life will place barriers before you that act as a surrogate daddy in the circumstances you face. It takes a godly dad to give influence, guidance, and assistance to identify and overcome these negative powers of influence in your life. Your life may have been shaped and influenced by events you experienced years ago that you have yet to acknowledge and reconcile.

So what are we to do? How are we to respond when we become aware of a negative behavior, physical characteristic, or tendency in us or our children that we have seen in previous generations? God's Word is true. Ignoring behavioral tendencies or denying them with the assumption they will go away on their own is naïve. Jesus said that knowledge of the truth would set us free (John 8:32). God's Word is true. When truth is coupled with open discovery and honesty, it brings us to revelation and understanding. Freedom comes when we recognize and renounce the behavior we have identified, and break its negative effect by the authority of God's Word working in our lives.

DIGGING THROUGH THE HEART

Many times during the early years of our marriage Jan and I noticed characteristics, tendencies, or behaviors in ourselves or our children and wondered where they came from and what the root cause might be. Sometimes as we discussed our individual responses to issues, Jan would point out an impact of my behavior on her. It wasn't an accusation; it was discussion about our individual behaviors. Jan would say, "At times you make me feel like I have to perform for you."

That statement evoked a defensive response from me. I thought her perspective was skewed and that she was seeing situations through fogged emotional glasses, projecting something on me that wasn't there. It was her problem, not mine. I had never asked her to perform for me! I was clean—wasn't I? Was it my behavior or her imagination? As long as I held to a defensive position of denial, I couldn't hear anything she was saying, let alone understand her feelings related to the impact of my behavior on her.

I have learned that when my response is defensive and invalidating, there is a very good chance that what has been identified is something that needs some further investigation. I received a breakthrough in this regard as I read Margaret Rinck's book. She said that when we explore issues of the heart, it is like going on an archeological dig. She went on further to write that when archeologists begin to dig in a site, they are extremely careful. When they uncover artifacts, they go to painstaking efforts of care with every item being unearthed. Using delicate tools and brushes, the archeologists unearth the artifacts. As they clean the artifacts, they go to extreme lengths to determine if they have something of value. All the effort is required because it is unknown if the item they have uncovered is a common earthen vessel or if it is a priceless vase or valuable work of artistry. Initially every item uncovered gets the same type of care and respect.

She went on to say this is the way it is to be when we uncover issues in our hearts. They must be uncovered with delicate care, respect, and patience. They must be handled with gentleness as they are exposed, processed, and categorized to determine their worth and influence on our lives.

Her explanation brought revelation to me, as it exposed a fear I didn't know I had at the time. I had given little thought to the impact of experiences from my past might have on me. I had learned to deny my feelings and move on. This response was a big part of my reaction to Jan when she questioned the emotional impact of issues on my life. I came to realize that my unwillingness to explore them was anchored in a fear that they would be mishandled.

I thought the method of digging up emotional issues from the past was going to be disrespectful and crude. I imagined it would expose things that were delicate and precious—still tender to me even though they were things that had happened years ago. I feared they would be treated lightly or made fun of as they were uncovered. Therefore, I thought they were best left alone. This thinking was all part of my subconscious security system designed to protect my heart. It kept my responses shallow and surface based: *What you see is what you get. It is what it is. There is no need to dig around in my heart. Things in the past needed to be left buried. My heart is fine—just don't mess with it.*

I used all these responses to Jan's attempts to help me discover and uncover issues in my heart. I saw Jan's questions as an unwelcome invasion, something like that of a tomb raider. They were insensitive and invasive. My answer was swift and definitive: "No, you can't dig around in my heart, and I won't either!"

This attitude began to change through the insight I received from Dr. Rinck's book. I decided to open my heart for a little exploration to see what was buried there and through a process of respectful care, seek an understanding of its impact on my life.

I'll pause here and say that as a pastor I knew the importance of a person's heart toward God; it is the place of His intimate work. The Bible tells us that we are to guard our heart because out of it flows our thoughts, our willful decisions, and our emotions (Prov. 4:23). These are the issues of life that impact our response to circumstances.

I thought my refusal to explore my heart was simply an act of guarding it. I did not see the discovery of experiences and their impact on my behavior as a valued part of the process of protecting my heart. It seemed to me that this process exposed your heart rather than protected it. I knew that God dealt with the issues of our hearts with sensitivity and care, but I needed to know that Jan would deal with me in this way as the issues in my heart were uncovered.

Let me also say that the Holy Spirit is a great partner when it comes to digging into the things that are held in our hearts. He is gentle, respectful, and noncondemning as He assists us in uncovering and processing all that our hearts hold secure. He will wait for our permission to explore and uncover things hidden there and, when granted, will be there to help give perspective about the memory and lead us to healing and freedom. This is exactly what happened for me.

A Pivotal Memory

Armed with a new perspective through Dr. Rinck's insight, I started to explore my heart. As I did, one of the first things I uncovered was a vivid memory from my childhood. It was not a repressed memory. It was not a memory I connected with hurt, pain, or trauma. It was simply an unprocessed memory from my childhood. I had no idea of its value to me or its impact on me. Like a discovery from an archeological dig, I carefully lifted it from my memory and began to dust it off to see what I had. I had not connected it in any way to the current behavior of my life, but as I brought it out for review, I received a whole new perspective.

The memory I began to process was one that involved my maternal grandmother. My family was very close to my mother's parents. They lived a few hours from us, and we saw them regularly. They were wonderful, giving, godly people.

They were a great influence and blessing to my parents and our family.

As I thought about them, my memories centered on a couple of characteristics reflected in the way I related to my grandmother. My grandmother was a woman with an aggressive way of relating, and she was a dominant influence in our family. When Grandma would come for a visit, my mom would muster my sisters and me like a drill sergeant preparing his troops for inspection. As we cleaned the house and made preparations, it was not unlike what you would expect for a visit from the president. We spent days cleaning everything—and I mean deep cleaning. All our hard work was offset by the knowledge that when Grandma arrived, if we passed her inspection, her approval would result in generous blessings in the form of special meals eaten out or a trip to the mall for some clothing purchases.

As I thought through this memory, it was not painful and there were no negative emotions evoked. As I reflected on my feelings about my grandmother and our times with her, a revelatory thought emerged, one that I had never connected with any of my current behavior. I began to see that I had developed an internalized concept in response to my grandmother's kindness and our preparations for her arrival. The revelation came as I recognized that what we were doing was demonstrating our love to her and for her through our performance. Our performance was represented in our preparation that was intended to please her. By pleasing her, we were telling her how much we loved her.

What became clear to me was that I had associated my concept of love with this type of performance. I even went a step further by connecting that loving performance with an expected benefit. It may not seem like a huge revelation, but it was eye-opening to me.

On the basis of that revelation I could clearly see the formula I had developed as I embraced this concept of love. I developed an expected response to my demonstrations of love. I had not ever consciously made that connection until I was processing this memory, but it became a revelation to me that through the expressions of love I was performing for Jan, albeit with good intention, I expected a reciprocal response.

As I carefully cleaned, lifted, and processed the revelation from this memory, I began to get clarity around its influence and impact on me. The things I did in preparation for my grandmother's visit were not done with any overt expectation of a specific benefit that we would receive. We did it because we loved Grandma and loved having her come to visit. However, the reality was that as I cataloged that expression of love for her, I interpreted her approval and generous response as the reciprocal payback for the work of love we had done in preparation for her arrival. I am not saying this interpretation was held by my mom or sisters, but it was held by me. It was my childish perception of what was happening at the time that created a formula of giving love and expecting a payoff.

When Jan and I got married, I carried that understanding and expression of love into our marriage. I performed sacrificial acts of kindness to demonstrate my love for her in practical ways such as vacuuming the house, doing the laundry, or buying her an extravagant birthday or anniversary gift, expecting a payoff in return. I attempted to pick up on little suggestions or subtle hints that gave an indication of something she wanted or desired so I could incorporate them in my responses of love to her. I was unaware that below the surface of my thinking lay the formula that had crystallized in my childhood and was being subconsciously applied to every act of love I made toward Jan—that by demonstrating my love through acts of service, she would reciprocate through appreciation and acts of generosity toward me.

On the surface of my thinking I knew it was wrong to expect a specific response to some loving act that I had done. That expectation would be wrong because it connected a selfish motive to a loving act that should have no strings attached. I knew love didn't give something to get something. True love gives expecting nothing in return. However, since I had no specific expectation attached to my actions, I thought my motive was pure and my acts of service were truly demonstrations of love.

I did not understand that an expectation, even if it is not specifically connected to a desired response, is still an expectation. So when Jan asked if I had any expectations, I told her no. There were times when Jan would point-blank ask me if I expected some response, and I would vehemently deny I had any expectations for how she would respond. In my mind I wasn't lying to her. I really was blind to the formula that was working in my subconscious. I stubbornly refused to acknowledge that I was expecting anything from her because I had no *specific* expectation of the kind of response she would give for what I did for her.

Let me pause here to process this with you. You may think as you read: "How could he not see this? How could he think that refusing to acknowledge an expectation would make it nonexistent?" I agree with you. It is crazy! If we are honest with each other as we talk through the pages of this book, though, we know that our response to the impact of circumstances is to go to extensive lengths to cover our hidden thoughts and deny our sin, rather than partnering with God to bring them to His light and healing.

So even though I denied any expectations at work in me, the formula at work in my subconscious caused me to wait with anticipation for a reciprocal response from Jan. The problem was that the reciprocal response often didn't come, or if it came I didn't connect it to one of my acts of love. When the formula of performance and reciprocal response remained unfulfilled, I felt hurt and rejected.

My internal conversation went like this: "I thought she loved me. I know she loves me! Then why does she not reciprocate my loving acts?" I concluded it was because of my performance—because the acts of love I did were not good enough—and I made an internal commitment to try harder, to be more expressive and more extravagant in my actions. I felt that by doing those things, I would surely bring the reciprocal response of approving appreciation and generous action from Jan that would complete the equation.

The problem with my formula was that it created an uncommunicated expectation that was so large (and it grew with every attempted act of love) that it could not be satisfied. It was an "expectation black hole" in my heart that swallowed up any act of approving appreciation or generosity made by Jan. The formula had a flaw, a circular loop, that allowed little or no satisfaction in any response she made toward me.

When this memory emerged from my heart, and with the Holy Spirit's help to bring its impact into clarity, I had an "aha" moment. What Jan had been describing as feeling like she had to perform for me (but which I had been denying and invalidating) was the hidden expectation that was part of this formula of love that was at work in the depths of my heart—a formula that said my performance would produce a reciprocal response of love and appreciation from her back toward me. Wow! She had been right all along! I did expect her to perform for me.

With this revelation clear to me, I could now make decisions that would produce change. The change was relatively simple compared to the process of discovery. First, I had to realize that an expectation in itself was not in itself wrong, while at the same time realizing any expectation that goes uncommunicated is wrong and hurts the relationship. Second, I had to openly identify and acknowledge my expectations. In some ways this involved a discovery process since I had gotten pretty good at hiding, camouflaging, and denying my expectations. I had to be open to Jan's questions related to my expectations and not respond with denial or defensiveness. Sometimes my honest response to her question was, "I don't know if I have an expectation or not. Let me think about it for a minute." Then as I looked into my heart and responded with what I found, she would help me process my response to a healthy place. Finally, I would openly and honestly share with her what I was thinking, feeling, and expecting. This type of honest communication is what opened the door for relational connection and intimacy.

Let's Talk About You

Who or what is responsible for the value system that drives your behavior? That is what is meant by the question, "Who's your daddy?" It may be something small from your childhood or it could be something major—something traumatic and hurtful that has dented the cylinder of your heart and impacts the way you process the issues of your life. It may be that you have adapted a *laissez-faire* attitude toward the internal responses you have made or are making to the circumstances you have encountered in your life. Either way, the impact and the full measure of their influence on your behavior may not be fully understood right now.

Whether you see it or not, the impact of past circumstances may have left some rough pieces that stick out in your subconscious and catch on the current circumstances of your life. They then influence your actions and reactions and magnify the passive-aggressive tendencies in your responses, as they did mine. If you will open your heart in willing partnership with the Holy Spirit, engaging in a process of exploring what is hidden, God will guide you in your exploration to a place of healing and wholeness.

Maybe your area of blindness has nothing to do with expectations. Maybe it is in a totally different area. The point is, until I became willing to explore my heart, my blindness remained. Today I see what I couldn't see for many years in our marriage. I never would have seen it if I had remained unwilling to open my heart and explore what was securely held behind the locked doors of denial and defensiveness in my heart.

What may be hidden in your heart that you are blind to today? Maybe it's not an issue of performance and expectation like it was for me. It could be a myriad of things that have happened and crystallized into a pattern of thinking that is affecting your behavior today. You see the fruit but don't know the root, just like I didn't know the root in my life. The reality is you won't know the root until you explore your heart as I did and discover—with the Holy Spirit's help—the impact of experiences and circumstances on your responses. You too will have to open your heart to the circumstances and issues that have been locked away in your heart in order to understand their impact and influence. I can tell you it is worth the work and it can be done in a safe way!

Chapter 6

I AM WOMAN, HEAR ME ROAR

⚜ JAN ⚜

HAVE BEEN OPINIONATED FOR AS LONG AS I CAN remember. When I see something happen or hear an idea expressed, I tend to immediately have an opinion about it. I don't wait to hear a lot of details, and I will freely give my opinion to anyone within earshot. I love a hearty discussion, so when I express an idea, I fully expect there to be an agreement or some type of debate regarding the issue. I love the process of sharing ideas, and debate and discussion energize me if done in a respectful manner. My desire to discover truth from different angles causes me to want to converse and openly discuss ideas. Further, when I share my thoughts aloud, it helps me to better understand the issue and how I feel about it.

This kind of interchange, however, is a "beat-down" to Tom. It is agonizing in every way because he wants to have a positive, peaceful discussion with a resolution at the end. When we were first married, I had thought Tom and I were totally on the same page in everything because he always seemed to agree with me. After we were married, it was confusing to me that there would be times when his actions didn't seem to line up with his words.

In trying to make sense of my confusion, I would ask him to explain his perspective. He would assure me that he agreed with my perspective, so I took him at his word. Although confused, I never thought his inconsistent actions meant he didn't agree with me. However, he was unwilling to discuss a controversial matter with me or to verbalize his disagreement on an issue for fear that it would lead to an argument. Because he shied away from discussions that ended in disagreement, he would often outwardly agree with me just to finish the conversation. The result was that many of our conversations were not satisfying to either one of us, yet we couldn't understand why.

The dynamic looked something like this. We would be having a conversation, and Tom would make a statement and I might disagree or offer another way to view the situation. I would give my thoughts and ideas about what he said and be looking forward to a dialogue (back and forth) about the issue, him giving his reasons for believing what he said and me giving alternative ways to look at it from my point of view. Maybe even a little tension would be involved in the discussion. I was OK with leaving the conversation with no resolution as long as we left with something to think about. All the while on his side, though, Tom would be trying to find a point of agreement or a way to resolve and end the conversation in peace and harmony.

I remember many conversations that started out as just an ordinary discussion until we came to a point of contention. Tom would state his position and I would state mine. He would contend for his position and I would contend for mine. The more I tried to get him to agree with me, the quieter he became. Then he would start nodding and saying, "Uh huh," so I would think, "See. He agrees with me, because if he felt differently he would still be voicing his difference of opinion." I would continue the discussion until I felt we came to an agreement.

I was clueless that I had hurt Tom in the way I was communicating to him. I noticed he was quiet, but he did not voice objections to what I was saying and I did not respect the passive way he wanted to communicate. I thought that eventually he would learn how to stand up for what he believed, and we would have lively discussions about it and we would both be happy. I did not realize there were things in me that were causing the breakdown in communication—things that needed to change.

One day as Tom and I were having a discussion, I had a revelation. We were sitting at the table and I was telling him my feelings about an issue. He was smiling and nodding his head in an agreeable way. That encouraged me to continue talking—until it hit me that though he was smiling and nodding, he wasn't saying anything. So I stopped and looked at him and said, "You don't agree with me, do you?" He looked surprised and sheepish and said, "Not really." So I asked, "Then why are you nodding and smiling?" He said, "Because I wanted you to know I was listening to you."

I was stunned. So this is what I had been dealing with all these years? I had assumed his nodding yes meant he agreed with me, but he only meant he was listening to me, not that he agreed. How many hours of conflict could we have avoided if we had figured this out years ago?

That simple act of stopping and asking a question changed our way of communicating. If I had not stopped and asked the question, I would still believe today that when he nods his head and smiles in a conversation, he agrees with me. I now stop when he is nodding and sometimes say, "You don't agree with me, do you?" And he is given the chance to state his feelings without having to contend with my intense forward momentum.

ARE WE WILLING TO CHANGE?

I've had to tamp down my emotions and listen to Tom if I truly want him to be engaged in the conversation. This is part of the give and take in our relationship. Tom has had to engage in debate more than he would want to, and I have had to calm down more than I would naturally. This is not a natural instinct for either one of us; it had to be learned and practiced. We do it out of respect for each other and for the health of our relationship.

Because I am passionate and intense when I'm communicating, I tend to ignore subtle signals in the conversation and push forward when warning bells are sounding and alarms are going off. In the passion of the moment I don't even hear them. I am talking about an issue and wanting a discussion but have used all the wrong methods to try to draw Tom out. The result is the opposite of what I want. It totally slows down the forward momentum of the conversation. Tom, for his part, will give short, noncommittal responses and might even try to change the subject. I will react to his passiveness and say something to try to stir him up to match my emotions. But no matter what I try, he is not going to engage in the heated discussion.

Then, after years of so many unsatisfying exchanges, Tom was given a book for staff development that described different communication styles. It talked about people with Tom's personality who like to have discussions in an orderly and peaceful way and how they enjoy having all the issues resolved and a plan in place when a conversation ends. For Tom's communication style, he needs to feel as though there will be little conflict or tension; otherwise he feels over-whelmed and shuts down emotionally. The result of his type of relating to me was that he always tried to bring our conversations to a tidy conclusion even if we hadn't fully discussed the issue to my satisfaction.

On the other hand, people with my personality type need a little heat—a spark and passion—in the conversation or we don't feel like the conversation was productive. We want to talk about issues because talking helps us hear what we think. We process by saying and hearing what we say. We don't need resolution from every conversation. There is satisfaction as long as we walk away with something to think about.

As I was reading the description of my style, I was excited to see there are other people like me. I ran into Tom's office and read him the page that dealt with my personality type and said, "See, I'm not wrong! There are other people like me. We need a little heat in our discussions. We want to toss ideas back and forth without resolving anything right away."

I continued on, saying, "It isn't wrong to feel the way I do. It is just different from you. You always want to end our conversations in your own peaceful way, but then I never feel like I've had a satisfactory conversation because you keep dumping water on the fire I am trying to start. I appreciate that you want a peaceful conversation, and that is fair, but I deserve to have some conversations my way too. Sometimes there will have to be a little heat and tension as a part of the conversation, and possibly nothing will be resolved at the end. I know this will be uncomfortable at times for you, but it will be satisfying to me."

And during this conversation, we both acknowledged that we had been closed-minded and judgmental regarding each other's communication needs. We made a commitment to consider the other person's needs as well as our own when we communicated. Our commitment that day to honor each other's communication style served as a catalyst to honesty and understanding in our communication.

Breaking Down the Female Factor

I shared in chapter 4 that women who are aggressive often have challenges in their relationships and are sometimes misunderstood and that the degree of a woman's assertiveness may range from mildly aggressive to dominant and controlling. It seems that if a woman is not quiet or passive, then she is labeled dominant. I define it like this: An assertive woman will speak her mind because she knows that her input is important and valuable. An aggressive woman will speak her mind because she wants to effect change and wants to be part of the process. A dominant woman will speak her mind because she thinks only her views are correct and wants to control the outcome of the situation. The range between assertive and dominant is quite wide and varied, and aggressive women cannot be lumped into one category.

Male discomfort

Men may feel dishonored dealing with an aggressive woman and may not be willing or able to interact with her. These men may be uncomfortable dealing with women for the following reasons:

- They may have been hurt or constantly over-ridden by women.

- They may have had a mother or authority figure who was domineering and insensitive to them.

- They may have had a girlfriend who took advantage of them.

In response to pain and hurt some men make the decision to never let a woman get the upper hand again. The list of reasons is infinite, but the result is that they are wary of dealing with aggressive women and tend to devalue and discount the aggressive woman in a relationship. If a husband has this tendency, he needs to uncover the hurt from the past that caused this attitude and be willing to deal with it in order to have a healthy partnership with his wife.

Female emotions

Another reason many men feel uncomfortable relating to women is that women react to issues so differently than men do. For example, women are often more emotionally expressive than men. We can get worked up emotionally about issues and sometimes may even cry. The "cry factor" often makes men uncomfortable and even unable deal with us. Their nature is to take care of issues in a logical way, but when women get involved in the discussion, it's possible things will get upended by the element of emotions. For some men emotions are illogical and slow things down; thus, they conclude it takes too much energy to involve women in their discussions. Further, men may feel confused and even angry when they think they are the cause of our tears. The result is that some men have decided to exclude women rather than embrace them and learn to appreciate their contribution.

Tears during a conversation were an issue for Tom and me early in our relationship. He and I would be talking about something and I might start to cry. He would notice I was crying and immediately stop the conversation to do whatever he could to fix things in the hope that my tears would stop. He was uncomfortable and totally bewildered as to why I was crying, so the conversation would turn from the original issue we were discussing to why I was crying. Not wanting to cause further hurt, Tom would end our conversation and begin to focus on my emotions and how to get past them. Ending the discussion wasn't my desire, but I didn't know how to help him to process my emotions and I couldn't help crying.

Emotions can be unpredictable and intense. Men and women may both cry about similar issues, but let's be honest: girls cry over things that wouldn't even occur to a guy to cry about. And there is no shame in crying. Crying is a way of dumping our emotions and is a healthy release of emotions. Crying does not make women weird or weaker than men.

In response to this perception some women have learned to stuff their tears, whether in a marriage, a friendship, or simply a meeting. It feels like tears are inefficient and slow things down when you are trying to get to a resolve. It is even embarrassing, since crying is only a release valve for you—no one else is helped by your tears! And they can lead to highly emotional discussions because tears are emotional. Plus, you feel so vulnerable when you cry, and tears are messy, ruin your makeup, and give you a headache. So why do it?

It's because sometimes your heart pops open and your eyes fill with liquid that can't be contained! As women, it is important that we learn how to handle our emotions so that they don't interfere with communication. But there also needs to be a place of freedom to be able to cry in a conversation without getting derailed.

It can make our husbands nervous and uber-sensitive when we respond to something they've said or done by crying. I remember one discussion that Tom and I were having where I just began to sob. Mortified, Tom stopped talking and just stared at me. He didn't want to say anything else that might upset me, so he said nothing. I looked at him and said, "I can't help the fact that I'm crying right now because I'm feeling very emotional, but I am interested in finishing this conversation, so could we still talk even though I'm crying?" Tom was tentative to continue, but we continued the conversation and I eventually quit crying. I was thankful he was sensitive to let me cry because I didn't want the crying to be a distraction from the issue, just an honest release of my feelings.

As women, it is important that we learn how to handle our emotions so that they don't interfere with communication. But there also needs to be a place of freedom to be able to cry during a conversation without getting derailed.

Some women have taken advantage of their husbands by crying to stop a conversation when it gets too hard or uncomfortable for them. This behavior is not fair or honest communication, and it is manipulative. It may bring temporary suspension of the discussion, but it does not foster healthy patterns of communication. Manipulation always creates barriers.

On the other hand, there are women who need to be encouraged to realize that crying is not a terminal condition to be avoided at all cost but that they can continue having a conversation even though they are crying. It is hard, messy, emotional, and may take a little more time to sort through things, but a conversation does not have to end just because of emotions and tears.

Feminist mistakes

Instead of appreciating and respecting the uniqueness of our different genders, many have looked down on or belittled the differences. Judgments and misunderstandings regarding gender differences only serve to bring further hurt and confusion into marriages. I think this is one of the reasons the feminist movement touched such a nerve in our country. It rose out of a feeling that women were being treated unfairly by men, and a movement began in order to change that perspective. While it may have started out with noble intentions, it has disintegrated into an anti-men, anti-family movement. In the feminist movement, the needs and desires of women have become more important than those of men or children. In elevating women, feminists have put down men and their uniqueness; in saying we are equal, they say we have no need for a man. These women have effectively stripped away the unique qualities each gender brings to the relationship in order to try to make us equal.

Because feminism has defined so much of who a woman should be and what she should look like, it is hard to discover what it means to be feminine. There is a big difference between being a feminist and being a female. Feminism doesn't acknowledge femininity at all. In fact, when I spell-checked the word *femininity*, guess what word came up? Feminism! Not femininity. Because we have learned feminism instead of femininity, we have a generation of women who don't know how to be strong, assertive women and yet still feminine. The feminist movement taught us to be strong and capable by trying to think and act like men. I say that on his best day even an effeminate man cannot think like a woman, and on her best day a masculine woman cannot think like a man. We are wired completely differently. If you are not afraid to look at the situation honestly, it is easy to identify the differences between men and women. They are both unique and wonderful, and should be respected for their strengths and differences.

In trying to make men and women equal in every way, we have lost the ability to see what a gift femininity is—both to men and women. The female gender is a God-given gender with unique physical, emotional, and even intellectual differences from the male gender. Anyone should realize there are far deeper differences than anatomical distinctions. It is these differences that have been misunderstood and have led us into an adversarial relationship with men instead of a partnership with them—where we each use our strengths to help each other. Both genders need to be valued and esteemed in order to create marriages and families that are successful and healthy. We need to accept that we are nothing alike but that we are made to complement each other, not to be like each other. By understanding we are different, we are able to celebrate each other and have compassion for each other. When we understand that men aren't wrong, that we were designed to be different and there is a good reason we are not the same, it puts us into a state of partnership rather than making us adversaries.

Competitive edge

Tom and I are both firstborns, and I'm sure that plays into the dynamic of our relationship. We both had the naïve outlook on relationships that there is a right way—a best way—to do marriage, and we each thought our own way was the best way. So we drove each other crazy trying to do it right, not in a balanced way but in a right versus wrong way! We each thought if we were right, then the other person was wrong, and we didn't see there could be situations where we both were right, just different. We have come to realize that "right versus wrong" thinking is destructive in a relationship because it puts us in a competition to prove who is right—and in a competition, there is a winner and there is a loser. If you are winning, then your spouse is losing. And in case you haven't figured it out yet, in marriage if one partner is losing, you are both losing. Marriage should be a win-win relationship.

If you will change the way you think about conflict and take it out of someone being right or wrong, you can begin to see your spouse as a partner, not an opponent. You can begin to make the changes you need in order to have a satisfying relationship—not by figuring out what is right or wrong, but by figuring out what works in your relationship.

LET'S TALK ABOUT YOU

Maybe, like me, you assumed your husband felt the same way you did, and finding out the reality is different than you thought may be very surprising and hurtful. Let me encourage you that even though the reality may be different than you thought, these differences don't have to end the relationship. It is important to understand and accept that your husband is very different from you. He doesn't feel the same way you feel about things, and he probably isn't going to react to your issues the same way you do—unless it is his passion too, and even then his expression of it may look different than yours. We can learn to appreciate the uniqueness of our husbands while also learning new ways of communicating with them. It is important for us to embrace and respect their differences in the same way we want them to embrace and respect ours.

Once I embraced the fact that Tom was not going to communicate the way I thought he should, I began to adjust my expectations in our conversations. Instead of feeling hurt and frustrated that he doesn't want to engage in a hearty discussion over issues, I now take his lack of response as a signal to me that I need to slow down and let him catch up to me. This takes practice and patience—and I am not good at either. I had to learn to become sensitive to his feelings and not justify running over them in my process of communicating.

When you are frustrated with your husband, it might be helpful to stop and remember the things that drew you to him in the first place. They may be the very things that are driving you crazy now. The thing that was so attractive to me about Tom was how he would listen to me, affirm me, and agree with my passion. Now, when I look closely, I can see that he never really engaged in the passion of my dialogue; he just listened and interjected things now and then. This left me free to be passionate and share openly with him.

Even when you have had a revelation on an issue that you have struggled with, it will take time to change the way you think and respond. You might think that things should turn around and start working immediately, but it takes time and effort to change thoughts and behaviors that have been an ingrained, unhealthy part of the marriage. Becoming aware of these behaviors and then being willing to change your thinking and actions is a significant step toward having the healthy marriage you desire.

Stopping to listen in the heat of the moment is very hard to do unless you realize this fact: the way you navigate these relational issues with your spouse is more important than the issues themselves. With every conversation, you are building a foundation in your marriage of trust and love. If you skip over the uncomfortable issues, it will eventually show up as cracks in the foundation of your marriage that make it susceptible to falling apart. Learning how to communicate with your spouse in the heat of conflict is crucial for the health of your marriage relationship. It may take a lot of time and practice—trying and failing and trying again. The reward is that you will lay a good foundation for your relationship to be able to connect with your spouse and create the relationship you want and need for a healthy marriage.

Chapter 7

NOW YOU SEE ME, NOW YOU DON'T

❧ TOM ❧

AVE YOU EVER PLAYED A GAME OF HIDE-AND-SEEK? Most of us played that game when we were children. A game of hide-and-seek is innocent fun for kids but becomes a threat to a marriage. As adults, we cannot use denial and avoidance to hide issues in our relationship. We cannot crouch in a corner, hiding our feelings and motives to avoid uncomfortable situations or as a means of coping with hurt and pain. If we do, we will foster an environment of subversive thinking. Our attempts to hide our real feelings and present ourselves as something we aren't ultimately erects barriers between us that prevent a deep connection in our marriage.

Denial seems to be a universal male trait that becomes exaggerated when dealing with passive-aggressive communication dynamics. Most men learn denial as they develop from boys to men. The development process teaches them to deny and avoid their feelings, adding varying doses of pride, arrogance, rejection, and invalidation as a means of developing toughness and independence in a boy on his path to manhood. The inadvertent by-product creates a barrier to connection and subverts the establishment of a true, intimate relationship with our wives later in life.

We need to change this development process for boys. We need to help men who have developed under these influences learn how to openly and appropriately express their emotions in relationships so they can connect with their wives in deep and meaningful ways. I am advocating for a balance in our emotional development and a healing from the wounds we received as boys. I am suggesting we change the way we view what is acceptable for men as we learn how to express ourselves and relate to our wives.

It All Began on the Playground

I learned to deny and suppress my emotions on my way to manhood, and maybe you did too. The emotional expressions of frustration, anger, and other negative emotions were discouraged from a variety of sources—family, friends, and influential adult figures in my life.

One of my earliest memories of an emotional expression that significantly shaped my development took place when I was in fifth grade. Every day at the noon recess the fifth-grade boys would play keep-away against the sixth-grade boys. The team holding the ball when recess ended got to begin with the ball the next day at recess. They also had bragging rights in the school for the time period they possessed the ball.

Since I was one of the biggest boys in the fifth grade, I was often called upon to "ice" the victory we were trying to secure. As time approached for the bell to ring, the smaller, faster boys would give the ball to me, expecting me to hold on to it against a gang of sixth-grade boys who were pulling, pushing, and grabbing in their attempt to wrestle the ball away from me (us) in the final minutes of recess.

One day this scenario was being played out, and I had the ball. I was holding on as tight as I possibly could while a mob of sixth graders were doing everything they could to pull the ball away from me. I knew it was minutes, maybe seconds, before the bell would ring. I held on as tight as I could, counting the seconds, desperately waiting for the sound of the bell. I could feel the ball being loosened from my grip, and I feared I might lose the ball and fail my fellow fifth graders.

In my panic I started screaming angrily and thrashing about in an effort to get the sixth graders away from me. My noise and reaction got the attention of one of the teachers monitoring the recess, and she blew her whistle. By the time she got there I was crying as I vented the panic and frustration I felt over possibly losing the ball to the sixth graders. As she attempted to understand what had happened, the bell rang and we were sent back to class. Through all the ruckus, we had remained in control of the ball despite my emotional outbreak—or maybe because of it—that was the good news. The bad news was that I had cried. Second and third graders cry, but not fifth graders!

Through situations like this the concept that "real men don't cry" was being impressed upon my masculine development. I had failed a development quiz on my road to manhood, and I had failed in front of the sixth grade boys—and on the playground for everyone to see! My failure taught me to avoid shame by denying my emotions. For the rest of the school year, my nickname was Crybaby Lane.

In response to the teasing and related shame I felt as a ten-year-old, I vowed no one would ever make fun of me like that again. I locked the door on my emotions. Not all my emotions, however. Laughter, joy, happiness—all the positive ones—were totally acceptable and allowed expression in my life. It was the expression of negative emotions such as anger, frustration, fear, insecurity, and disappointment that I locked away. Any circumstance that evoked those emotions were met with denial and reflected in statements such as, "I don't care," "It doesn't bother me," "I didn't feel that," or "That didn't hurt me." All were the growing expressions of denial rooted in my playground experience from fifth grade.

Skimming Along the Surface of Truth

A few years later my newly formed habits of denial were refined further as I learned how men relate to women. I was dating Jan Frazier, this amazing girl I had known since junior high, but now she was my girlfriend. I wanted to learn how to relate to her in a loving and caring way with marriage as the ultimate goal. As our dating relationship progressed, I became involved with her family and the activities they shared.

One of her family's favorite activities involved boating. They had a boat and enjoyed going to the lake for fun family time together. I began to be included in their day excursions to a regional lake where they boated. I loved the lake and all the fun activities—skiing, tubing, enjoying picnic lunches, and playing games on the beach. In every activity I wanted to present myself as accomplished, classy, and a real man, worthy of Jan's affection and her parents' approval. I was developing in my concepts of manhood and in every possible circumstance trying to live by the macho code, "Never let 'em see you sweat."

It didn't matter if I had never done something before; it didn't matter if I felt out of control while doing it or if I got hurt when doing it. The code said you were to remain calm and never reveal the true nature of what was going on inside, regardless of your inner turmoil.

Jan's dad was a great man and definitely someone I wanted to impress. He usually drove the boat when we went skiing, but his boat-driving was a little scary. When you were skiing, he would pull the ski rope around for you to grab, and when the rope was getting tight between you and the boat, without warning, ready or not, he would push the throttle down—you were coming out of the water, with or without your skis! In fact, he was so consistent in this move that our family now refers to it as the "grandpa pull," signifying that unexpected moment when you nearly get your arms torn off as you are yanked out of the water!

When we were at the lake back in those days, if we weren't skiing, we were tubing. Today there are some really great tubes for pulling behind your boat, big ones you can lay flat on and L-shaped ones you can sit in like a recliner as you're chauffeured around the lake. It wasn't that way when we began tubing. All we had was a large rubber inner tube from a semitrailer tire that was inflated and a rope tied around it so it could be pulled behind the boat. The tube had a long metal stem coming out of the center that was designed to stick through the truck's rim; it also gave the tube support for inflation. They were dangerous for tubing because of the stem and the damage it could do as you laid on the tube and were hauled behind the boat at supersonic speed. The ultimate goal of tubing was to see how long it took for you to be thrown off the tube, creating the most spectacular kaleidoscope of events possible for the entertainment of all who were watching from the boat.

When we were tubing, Jan's dad drove the boat consistent with the way he drove it for skiing. When the rope was nearly tight between you and the boat, it didn't matter if you were on the tube, ready or not, he was going to push the throttle down—so you'd better be securely on the tube with a tight grip or it would be a short ride!

With a tight grip, you might be able to hold on as the boat picked up speed and you were slung from side to side (this was done with the full intention of throwing you off). All this action created excitement and pleasure for those watching from the boat. The goal was to create, at the very moment you were thrown off, a response of *oohing* and *aahing*, followed by the tension of a momentary gasp, where all in the boat waited for you to surface from under the water to see if you survived. When you surfaced, there would be relieved laughter and responses such as, "That was awesome—you rolled four times after you fell off!" "It looked like your arm was ripped off—are you OK?" and "Want to go again?" That last question demanded an answer, and this was the moment at which the macho code rose up. It didn't matter if you had the breath knocked out of you as you rolled across the surface of the water four times. It didn't matter if you couldn't raise the arm that almost got ripped off as you were flung off the tube—you still had the use of the other arm. Despite your condition, no matter what you were feeling and short of being knocked out, you rode one more time. The code demanded it.

The reason you said yes was because of the shame you'd experience if you didn't ride again—from the sarcastic comments that would come from those on the boat. They would ask questions such as, "Was it too much? We can give you a sissy pull instead!" If you showed any hesitation or admitted any hurt, they would say something such as, "Wah, wah, do we need to call the Wahmbulance?" Their taunting demanded another ride, and their statements necessitated a response—regardless of your condition—that went something like this: "Oh, absolutely! I want to go again—and this time, try and make it go fast. Come on, show me what ya got!"

One time I was thrown off the tube, and in the process the stem scraped my stomach and rib cage as I was bounced around and ultimately thrown off the tube. It was a spectacular spill that flung me off the tube to the delight and enjoyment of all the family and friends on board. I surfaced to *oohs* and *ahhs* and laughter, then response from the guys in the boat. I felt the sting of what I thought was a surface scratch from the tube stem, but I mounted up to go again. I wanted to avoid any ridicule, despite the fact that I was hurting from being thrown off the tube.

It wasn't until I got back into the boat and took off my life jacket that we all saw a bleeding cut on my stomach and chest. To my male friends, it was a battle scar, but to Jan and the other women, it was a call to go easier on those tubing, and they gave me sympathy and compassion for my injuries. Both responses touched something in my emotions. My male friends gave me respect and honor; Jan and the other girls gave me tender, affectionate care.

Experiences like this cemented a pattern of denial in my life and closed off my emotions, which hindered my ability to connect with Jan on issues that impacted our lives.

A Locked Door

Jan expressed herself with passion and emotion, which I interpreted as excessively dramatic. I felt ill equipped to know how to connect with her emotions, and they made me uncomfortable. My responses were subdued, passive, and closed, which I felt were consistent with the male code. My experiences had convinced me that expressions of emotion and passion were signs of weakness in men and weirdness in women. The best I could do was to passively listen. I couldn't relate, connect, or offer any meaningful interaction.

This did nothing to deepen our marriage connection. Jan was a passionate, expressive woman trying to connect with me on issues. I was a passive man in denial of my emotions. Connection was difficult and frustrating for both of us. Jan would make many attempts to draw out my emotions and feelings on issues—with little satisfaction. She would watch me as I navigated through a difficult situation and ask, "How did that make you feel?" Or she would ask me an even more paralyzing question: "What are you feeling right now?" Because of the locked door of my emotions, my response was always, "I don't know." If she continued on, suggesting that I pause a moment and get in touch with my feelings, I would respond, "Why?" I would go on to say, "If I get in touch with them, it won't change anything. It is what it is."

My emotional Fort Knox had a sign on it that read "No one allowed!" Not even me. With no one allowed, there was no deep intentional connection on emotional issues between Jan and me regarding circumstances that impacted our lives. This lack of emotional intimacy caused a barrier that neither of us wanted yet my denial kept in place.

A CLOSE CALL

When our children were young, we belonged to a neighborhood swimming pool. We would often take the kids swimming in the evening after work or on the weekend during the heat of the afternoon. One Sunday afternoon we made our way to the pool. We checked in and I took our son, Todd, to the locker room to change. Jan assumed that Lisa, our younger daughter, who was about four, had gone with us to the locker room. When Todd and I emerged without Lisa, Jan asked where she was. When I said I didn't know, she turned her attention in a panic toward the pool, scanning the crowded water looking for Lisa.

Then she saw Lisa lying on her back, several inches under the water, right below the lifeguard stand. She jumped in and lifted Lisa to the surface of the water, flipping her over in one swift move while still in the pool so she could pound on her back to expel all the water Lisa had swallowed. Although it was a matter of seconds, it seemed like an eternity before Lisa finally coughed, began spitting up water, and gasped for a breath. In the seconds that had transpired I was confused watching Jan jump into action. When it became clear that Jan was responding to a drowning situation with Lisa, I jumped in the water with them and carried a coughing, crying Lisa out of the pool, wrapped her in a towel, and then placed her in Jan's arms to be comforted. Jan was in complete shock over what had just happened. She was going through the motions in an automatic response.

It was unbelievable that Lisa had almost drowned in those few minutes. Yet true to the nature of my denial over emotional issues, I made a quick assessment of things. All appeared to be good. So I said to Jan, "OK, since all is good, I'm going to take Todd in for a swim." Lisa was still in Jan's arms crying, but she was breathing and all was good—by my shallow assessment. My denial told me the crisis was over, the catastrophe had been avoided, and life could go on as before. No need to pause and process the emotional trauma we had just experienced.

I was in denial, but Jan was in shock. She was stunned by what had just happened and even more stunned by my reaction to the tragedy we had narrowly avoided. In a controlled but passionate tone, she said, "If we don't leave right now, I am going to lose it right here in front of everybody. You better not go anywhere but to take me home."

So we gathered our belongings and walked out of the pool with many eyes on us as we left. When we got home, Jan went immediately to the bedroom and cried her eyes out while I sat in the living room entertaining our kids. I didn't know exactly how to relate to her emotions. All was well, wasn't it? Lisa was alive and acting normal. What was there to process? We can move on—we're good, right?

Jan finally came into the kitchen and sat down to eat with us. Todd asked her why she was crying. She told him that mommies just cry sometimes. He said, "Oh, I thought it was because Lisa almost drowned."

There you go—our young son was more in touch with the whole situation than his dad!

I was paralyzed by denial and unable to act with sensitivity and support for my wife. I was clueless and blind to the impact of the emotional circumstances we had just been through. My family and I had been emotionally impacted by the event, but deep-seated denial was standing in the way of my ability to acknowledge that reality. Even more tragic was my inability to connect with my wife over such an emotionally impacting event in our family.

Then Came Golf

After I graduated from college, while we were in the early years of our marriage, we lived in Oklahoma City. We became involved in a church and developed some very close friendships with young couples our age who also had children the same age as ours. We grew in our relationship with God and our friendships while living there, but it was a disconnected time in our marriage. I was new in my career so I was working long hours. We had one car that I drove to work, leaving Jan stranded in our apartment with two young children.

On top of that I was very selfish. When my male friends from our church would ask me to play golf on Saturdays, I would accept without talking to Jan. I knew if I asked Jan, she would object, having been cooped up in the apartment all week with two kids and without a car. I instinctively knew her objection would turn into hurt and anger because of my insensitivity. But that didn't stop me. I played golf almost every Saturday.

Jan interpreted my selfishness and desire to be with my guy friends as a decision to not be with her and the kids. How could she see it any other way, right? But I didn't feel that way at all. I told myself I just needed some guy time. I thought I could accommodate both. It was to me like having my cake and eating it too. I justified my selfishness by thinking it would be OK since I was going to play golf early in the morning and would be home by the afternoon to spend the rest of the day with her and the kids.

I sought to avoid the conflict I knew would develop between us by not involving her in the decision. I naïvely thought that by keeping her in the dark about my plans until the last minute, I would avoid conflict between us. Often I wouldn't even be the one who told her about my plans—she would hear it through a comment from one of the guys or find out through a conversation with the wives. My foolish attempt to avoid conflict resulted in hurting Jan through my insensitivity, selfishness, and dishonesty. In the end conflict wasn't avoided at all.

One day Jan said to me, "I don't think it's fair for you to be gone every day and then be gone a half-day on Saturday." Rather than recognizing her point and appreciating her commitment to our family, I thought she was coming against my chance for relaxation and fun after a full and busy week. She was simply pointing out that we had very little time as a family. She wanted input into the decision of whether I would play golf or not, but I protested by telling her the guys would think I was henpecked if I told them I had to get her permission before I could give them an answer. Pride kept me locked into a response of avoidance and selfish insensitivity. Rather than embracing a process of partnership that included my wife on issues that impacted our family, I avoided the uncomfortable conversations that were needed to bring us to connection and agreement.

After a few months of this process of avoidance, denial, and selfishness, we sat down to discuss my attitude, which had developed into an elephant in the room. I negotiated a deal—I am sure that is what it felt like to Jan—that allowed me to play golf with my friends two times a month.

But partners don't negotiate. They communicate, compromise, and support each other's vision and desires as they work together toward common goals.

I thought I was choosing the best course that would minimize our conflict as I withheld information from her, lied to her, and then defended my behavior when she desired to have a say in the schedule commitments I made that impacted our family. I justified it to myself, but it was a terrible miscalculation based on the deception working in my life, one that had no good effect on the intimacy and connection in our relationship.

It Comes Down to Denial and Avoidance

I have seen this process of denial or avoidance repeated by other men in their marriages with equally negative results. Why would we think that by withholding information, lying, or relating through contentious, defensive communication, we could avoid conflict? The answer is because we are blinded by denial. Further, through denial we allow avoidance to build a barrier that hinders our connection. Avoidance is no more our friend than denial; it must also be stripped of any influence in our lives.

Avoidance can take the form of insensitivity to circumstances, like it did with me that day at the pool or in the way I made plans for golf without consulting Jan. It can also be a response to conflict in your relationship. Conflict creates drama that impacts our emotions. While denial seeks to control the impact of the drama by minimizing its influence, avoidance seeks to bypass the emotions developed from the drama through lying, hiding important details, and circumventing the process of open, honest dialog. We do this in the false belief that our actions will keep conflict from happening. In the short term we may be able to delay the conflict by our efforts, but in the long term avoidance will limit our connection with our spouse and stifle intimacy from developing in our marriage.

Many men are not willing to come to grips with their emotions. Nor are they willing to take the steps necessary to open the emotional door in their lives. Instead, they choose the lesser expression of denial and avoidance, believing that to be a true expression of manhood. Please don't settle for this response. It only allows the barrier of disconnection to remain in your marriage.

LET'S TALK ABOUT YOU

If you have closed yourself off to passion and emotion, isn't it time for a change? If there is a barrier between you and your wife that is preventing the connection you desire, don't give up! Denial may be the culprit, but it can be removed. Your avoidance may be adding to the disconnection you feel, but it too can be booted out of your relationship.

Start by opening the door to the emotions in your life. Debunk the motto of macho manhood that was given to you as you grew up. Accept a new definition of manliness. Stop giving denial a place, and open your heart for discovery and expression. Discover what's in your heart by asking and answering questions such as, "How did I feel when...?" or "What was I thinking when...?" Push through the conflicts that may arise as you learn to express yourself honestly. Partner with your wife in this endeavor. Your combined efforts will bring down the barriers that have developed, making way for a new and deep connection to come into your relationship.

Chapter 8

THE "S" WORD

⨯⨭ JAN ⨮⨯

N THE SIX DECADES I HAVE BEEN ON THIS EARTH, I have come to the conclusion that I really don't like religion. Don't be shocked—I'm a pastor's wife and I love the church and I love people, but what I find distasteful is what religion represents: a set of roles and rules that you need to follow to get God's approval. I don't believe God's love for us is dependent on our responses. He doesn't love us more if we are following all the rules and getting it all right. He loves us no matter what because His nature is love. He gave us instructions for right living because He knows what is best for us. He is the one who made us and understands everything about us, and He knows what will give us the greatest opportunity for succeeding in life.

What religion says to me is that if you follow these certain rules, God will love you. If you don't follow them, God will hate you. Religion makes us a pretentious people! It is not about being religious—it is about the heart. Religion is a burden for us to live up to. Religion has God all figured out and packaged up nice and tidy. It makes people feel like there is something they can do to earn God's love. However, having a relationship with God is nothing like that. Relationships are not nice and tidy; they are messy and will have ups and downs, but we are always pursuing Him and growing and learning about Him. It's about having a growing, loving relationship with the Creator.

So when I talk about submission in this chapter, I want to do it in a way that doesn't sound religious. I want you to hear it through ears that have not been hurt by teachings or sermons that have disheartened and confused you. I know that for many of us, submission has become "the S word." I hope to give you encouragement about what God is teaching you about having a good marriage through the practice of submission.

What It Doesn't Mean

If you've been in the church for very long, you've probably heard this statement: "The husband is supposed to be the head of the home." Many people think that is what the Bible says. In my early years of learning about how to be a godly wife, I was certainly taught that the husband is supposed to be the head and leader of the home, the priest and king of the castle.

As I shared in an earlier chapter, this means I began to believe I was supposed to let Tom lead in everything—every decision and any direction for our family. Although I stayed home with the kids and felt I had a good perspective on things, he needed to make all decisions. So when a decision needed to be made, I would give him input, then he would make the decision and I would submit.

When Tom wasn't leading like I thought he should, I would point things out to him that needed attention and try to urge him to take the lead. I had ideas about what needed to be done, and Tom just didn't see things like I did. When he didn't lead, I would be frustrated with him for not being a good leader.

An issue would come up that he needed to take care of, so I would pray and pray about it and leave it in God's hands like I thought a submissive wife should. When he did nothing about it, the thing that I was afraid might happen *did* happen, and I would be upset with Tom for not leading like he was supposed to. It seems silly now, this trying to position myself in a place that wasn't even intended for me, but I was trying to do things the right way.

Then one day a good friend and I were talking at lunch, and she was sharing about what damage has been done in homes and marriages through incorrect teachings regarding submission. She said that sometimes men are good, strong leaders, but sometimes they are not. Maybe the wife is naturally a better leader, but if she believes her husband is supposed to lead then she is putting a burden on him he is not equipped to handle. His gifting is not in leadership, yet he is being put in that position. When he doesn't lead effectively and she knows what should be done, she may get frustrated with him or try to push and prod him into action. This causes friction between them, and she finds herself constantly frustrated and disappointed that her husband isn't taking the leadership role he should take in their home. Neither one of them ends up satisfied with the role they have been given.

There is also a school of thought that says as the head of the home, the husband should handle all the finances. This is fine as long as he is a good money manager. But when he does not know how to handle money well, there can be disastrous consequences.

If the woman is more gifted in handling money, let her handle it. If she is a better leader, let her lead. There should be mutual respect and recognition, not competition, for our unique gifts and talents. If you look around at successful marriages, you will find couples that have figured out what works for them. They are not weighed down by the rules and roles that others try to put on them.

WHAT IT DOES MEAN

This teaching of the husband being the head of the home is distorting what the Bible actually teaches about the authority structure in the home. Ephesians 5 starts out by telling us to follow God's example and walk in the way of love. Verse 21 gives a description of how this should function in the home. It says we should submit to each other in respect and love for God. The next verses say wives are to submit to their husbands because the husband is the head of the wife. It doesn't say he is the head of the *home*, as many people think. He is the head of his *wife*. This means our husbands are in the position of being our head or our covering—our protection. We submit to them as an acknowledgement of their position of authority in our lives and as a faith response to God's order in marriage.

The passage then states that husbands should love and cherish their wives as Christ loved us and gave Himself for us. It says a man's attitude should be one of sacrifice for his wife and that this is how a healthy, faith-filled home functions best. It never instructs the husband to *be* the head of the wife. Instead, it says he *is* the head of his wife. It's not something he has to do; it something that just is. I cringe when I hear a man say to his wife, "You need to submit to me because I'm your husband." That tells me something is off in their relationship. We are partners in marriage and look out for each other's best interest. Understanding this key point will help to lay the foundation for a real, healthy, and successful relationship.

My problem was that I tried to do things that looked like submission but were totally not me. I tried to imitate women who were held up as examples of submissive women, but they were nothing like me. They were usually quiet and compliant, and I couldn't even relate to that. I began to carry a weight of frustration and disapproval, feeling as if I was screwing up all the time. I worried that what I was doing would not look like submission and would not please God.

This kind of thinking brought me into a loop of worry, performance, and failure. I was failing to live up to a standard, so I tried harder to succeed. After multiple failures I carried a heaviness in the back of my mind at all times—a heaviness that said I was disappointing my husband, others, and God. This did not have a positive impact on my life.

I think there are really good teachings on being submissive to our husbands, but there are also wacky ones that do not reflect the heart of God. If you feel you are constantly failing and defeated, I can assure you that is not what God is saying to you. Our situation is never hopeless when God is speaking. When God speaks, there is always encouragement, affirmation, and a way to fulfill His desire without feeling squashed like a bug. When you hear a teaching, it may bring about conviction and a desire for change, but a true teaching will always bring a feeling of hope and affirmation if it is from God. If our desire is to follow God and do things His way, He will not make us feel unworthy or unable. He brings encouragement and peace in the process.

The key to understanding submission is realizing it is a basic principle of life. We are all under authority of some kind and are required to submit, like an employee to a boss, like a citizen to a policeman, like a student to a teacher, or like a taxpayer to the IRS. We all have areas of our life we have to submit to someone.

Why is submission important in marriage? It is the key to unity and harmony in human relationships. From the beginning of time God set up an authority structure so that He can work out His will on earth and in our lives effectively. Submission to our husbands has to begin with submission to God. If we do not understand the authority of God and Scripture, it is not likely that we will be able to submit to our husbands. It is the kind of thing that requires faith and respect as we let someone else have the final say in the decisions that affect our lives.

WHAT DOES AUTHORITY HAVE TO DO WITH IT?

Learning to submit to authority should begin when we are children. We learn to obey our parents, teachers, policemen, and others. When children are taught the concept of submission to authority, they find it easier to submit later in life. If we don't understand the importance of submission ourselves, it will be hard to teach it to our kids. I had a relationship with God from an early age and I learned to listen to His voice and to obey Him, but I didn't understand the concept of authority. Even though I loved God, I did not understand submission in marriage (the good and bad of it) until later in my marriage.

I grew up in the sixties, and rebellion was encouraged. It was quite a popular idea to challenge authority. I remember a few of our teachers in high school even encouraged us to debate with them on issues. It was like a rite of passage into adulthood. Submission was not respected or valued in our culture. Self-expression was. I personally had no trouble at all submitting to authority—as long as I agreed with it. But

I was not afraid to challenge the rules if I thought they were unreasonable. I wasn't the kind of kid who was rebellious and despised authority, but I definitely didn't have a clear understanding of authority or what my attitude should be toward the authority figures in my life.

I brought this ignorance of what authority looked like into my marriage. When I began hearing about a wife's role of submitting to her husband, I had no life experience to compare it to, so my reaction was often confused and resentful toward the teaching and toward Tom. Being a woman of faith, I understood obedience to God. But as an assertive woman, figuring out what submission to my husband looked like was confusing.

Submitting to one's husband begins with submitting to God. The heart of submission is really trusting in God—that He is in control, that He knows us, that He knows what is best for us, and that He will take care of us. When we understand submission to God's ways, that He loves us and wants the best for us, submission becomes comfortable and rewarding.

Ultimately we need to know that submission isn't about changing our personalities. Rather, it's about a posture we carry in the relationship toward the other person. God created us with different personalities and different strengths and weaknesses. Some people have strong personalities, and some have more compliant personalities. You may have often noticed that a strong, assertive personality seems to have a harder time submitting to authority than a quieter, compliant one does. Their actions are out there for everyone to see. But you can't always judge from outward appearances. If you have observed people for very long, you realize that some very quiet, seemingly compliant people are not really submissive at all!

They just quietly and subtly do things their own way—it's just not as obvious to those around. Submission is an attitude of the heart, and it doesn't always look the same in every person.

Submission means realizing we can be ourselves, but we are choosing not to have the final say in the outcome. It means acknowledging someone else has authority over us. In our marriage, that is our husband. He is our authority. Again, this system was not set up by God to imprison us but to protect us. It's not set up because we're imbeciles and our husbands are brilliant either, or because we're not capable or are inferior. God gave us this structure for the simple fact that every institution that exists has to have structure to be able to function effectively and thrive. Marriage is no exception.

What If You Disagree?

So, if we are to submit to our husbands, will that mean we never disagree on things? Don't be ridiculous—of course you will disagree! If you agreed on everything, one of you would be unnecessary. Disagreement is not the issue. It is *how* we disagree that can bring strife and division. If you are a passionate woman, then you probably disagree passionately. Often we react to our husbands out of our passion, which may be intense. But understand this. A reaction is our initial response. It's unfiltered and uncontrolled. Our goal, however, is to learn to *respond* to what is being said or done versus *reacting* to it. This means taking a minute to evaluate what has been said before we react. The difference between reaction and response is stopping to think. I'm still working on that.

Part of having a submissive heart is giving up the need to always be right. For those of us who think our way is always the best way, it usually takes some convincing for us to see that another way may also be acceptable. But we can learn to stop, step back from the situation, and see things from our husband's perspective.

Submission does not mean you just stop the discussion and say, "You're right. I will obey." That is not true submission. A true relationship with God and your husband involves a dialogue back and forth. What submission requires is that you respect your husband when you disagree with him. You may have a valid point or you may be totally correct in your perspective, but part of the process of being a helper to your husband is giving him input that he can receive without being demanding. You may even discover that he has a better perspective than yours! If we have a heart of submission, our husbands will feel safe with us and will be able to listen to what we have to say.

Every marriage has its own dynamics and is very unique because of our different personalities and the different stages of marriage we are in; thus, submission will look a little different in every relationship and at every stage. Learning to properly communicate our feelings in love and respect is the key to growing together. By realizing that submission to our husbands is God's idea, we can willingly learn how to do that in our marriage.

LET'S BE REAL ABOUT CONTROL

Not only is submission giving up the need to be right, but submission is also about giving up control. For many women, quietness and trust are the hardest qualities to attain. We feel strong and secure when we are able to manage our lives and surroundings and when things are going our way. I think it is important to identify what controlling tendencies look like. You might be controlling if:

1. People tell you you're controlling.

2. You get angry when things don't always go your way.

3. You lash out at people who disagree with you.

4. You try to change the people around you against their will.

5. You cannot stand to be challenged by anyone.

6. You withhold affection from and give the silent treatment to people you are angry with.

7. You feel obligated to tell others what is wrong with them yet cannot listen to criticism of yourself.

8. You always think your way is the only way to do things.

I think many of us deal with issues of control. These tendencies can come out in anyone, and we may not even realize we're being controlling. But if we don't recognize that we have control issues, we won't be able to relate to our husbands in a healthy way. Our goal is to have submissive hearts. We want our husbands to trust that we will be real and truthful with them and will trust them with the outcome of the decisions we make. We freely choose to take a position of submission to our husbands to honor their place in our lives. We need to get past the question of who is the boss and see the bigger picture. Though we are equal with our husbands, we voluntarily lay that equality aside in order to honor God and our husbands.

Love is the ultimate motive for submission. If our submission involves any fear other than the fear of God, we need to recognize it and deal with the issues that are causing the fear. These could be fear of rejection, fear of conflict, fear of displeasing, fear of abuse, fear of failure, or any number of other fears.

We take positions under our husbands to express our trust in God and love for them. It is difficult to trust someone who is imperfect, but our trust will grow as we see how God works in our marriage. Our trust grows as we communicate with and listen to the words and the hearts of our husbands. To truly know another person and learn to trust him through submission, we must be willing to communicate our inner thoughts, feelings, motivations, and values to each other. Trust only grows in an environment of commitment. It grows in an atmosphere of faithful reassurance. It thrives in open and honest communication.

LET'S TALK ABOUT YOU

As I've stated, submission was a confusing issue for me. How are you doing with the issue of submission in your life? Does the word *submission* give you a knot in your stomach or make you angry? It is possible to feel afraid of submission if you don't understand the heart of the issue. Do you understand or honestly believe God will work in your life through your heart of submission? It can be terrifying or liberating, depending on your perception of what God is asking of you.

You have the opportunity to have a peaceful, successful marriage if you will be diligent to learn the truth about submission. While peace is our ultimate goal, we cannot get there by keeping silent. Is there good, honest communication in your marriage? Are you able to express your perspective along with your concerns over the situations you and your husband are facing? Remember, pretending to go along with things on the outside that you don't support on the inside is not submission. True submission is about honestly communicating your feelings and desires to your husband and then yielding your right to have things done your way. As you learn to walk in this way, it is amazing how much peace it can bring into your life and into your marriage.

Chapter 9

WHICH DOOR WILL YOU CHOOSE?

❧ TOM ❧

WHEN I WAS GROWING UP, *LET'S MAKE A DEAL* was a popular game show on TV. Its host, Monty Hall, would offer a panel of contestants an opportunity to trade an item they had brought to the show for an item he was offering. If they made the trade, the contestant may receive something of greater value, but he also risked the possibility of ending up with something of little or no value. At the end of the show the contestant with the highest value trade was offered one final trade opportunity. Behind one of three curtains on the stage was the show's grand prize. The contestants could pick one of the three curtains or keep the sure prize they had in their hand. The tension grew as the person thought about risking the known for the unknown. The audience cheered as the person looked to family and friends to advise him on the right decision. Would he trade the new kitchen appliances he had in his possession for the possibility of winning the grand prize behind one of the curtains? The grand prize could be a new car—or it might be a children's stroller. Both items were transportation of sorts but only one was the true grand prize. That was the dilemma and the risk.

Some couples approach their marriage as if they are contestants on *Let's Make a Deal*. They process the circumstances of their lives as if they are making trades in the hope of ultimately being lucky enough to end up with the grand prize package in their marriage relationship. As their life moves forward, it holds opportunities and choices that require decisions that will impact their happiness. They feel the tension associated with making the right choice, just as the contestants did on the show. Their focus is making sure their choice will result in their securing the prize that benefits them and their relationship the most. They look to others for help and encouragement to assist them as they trade through the circumstances of life on the way to hopefully securing the grand prize of marriage satisfaction.

The problem with this approach, however, is that marriage is not a game. It is serious business with generational consequences. Marriage directly impacts the legacy we leave to our children and grandchildren.

The circumstances we face serve as opportunities to learn and grow in our understanding of God's ways. A contestant in a game show is focused on winning the prize, but as believers our focus is on understanding God's work in the situations we are encountering. Our goal is not to progressively improve our circumstances through lucky choices but to experience God's love as we work through every situation, knowing that as we experience Him, we will experience contentment, satisfaction, and peace.

Keeping a contestant mentality can lead us to trade out of our circumstance before experiencing God's desires or receiving, through our pursuit of Him, a greater understanding of His ways. We make choices we think will enable us to escape the discomfort and disappointment of our immediate circumstances rather than focusing on the pursuit of God's heart and perspective over the dilemma we face. Some situations we deal with take us through multiple cycles of hope-filled anticipation only to lead us to disappointment when our expectations go unmet. Multiple cycles of anticipation followed by disappointment produce disillusionment and frustration and can lead to a loss of a perspective of faith in the situation. In desperation we may be tempted into "contestant thinking." The compassion and care of our family as they watch us struggle may lead them to support us in this way of thinking. The temptation is to identify and then pick an option available to us that offers the hope of being delivered from the unhappiness of our current circumstances without further work, hurt, or disappointment.

DOOR NUMBER ONE: A CLEAN START

In this chapter we're going to look at three potential responses to the struggles we face in our marriages—three "doors," if you will, that we can choose as we are faced with the tension of what to do. The first door we'll discuss is divorce.

I've seen this door chosen many times, so let me share with you a few stories. One couple was on the road of hurt and wounded expectations when they came to see me. Their marriage was in crisis. We knew the couple well because our lives had been intertwined for several years through church activities and family connections.

This couple was coming to see me in a desperate move to address critical problems in their marriage. Neither had been unfaithful, but both were unhappy and unsatisfied with the lack of connection and fulfillment in their marriage. They had experienced multiple cycles of hopeful anticipation followed by the deep disappointment of unmet expectations resulting from their failed efforts. Discouraged and disillusioned, they looked for the answers that had eluded them. They looked to me for a biblical perspective on their problems, as they were on the verge of resorting to "contestant thinking." They were searching for the option that would lead them to the curtain with the dream marriage behind it. They were disappointed that the work they had put into their relationship had not produced what they were looking for, and they were tempted to think there was a luckier choice that might get them what God and their efforts to this point had failed to produce.

Their marriage was in serious jeopardy, and I gave them practical steps to guide them toward a solution. But the amount of effort required and the time it would take to implement the solution I gave them led them to pick another option. In response to hurt and disappointment they chose door number one.

Door number one is the door with divorce hidden behind it. They thought they could trade in their problems for a clean start in a new relationship, as they hoped to find the grand prize of a dream marriage. But they failed to consider all the implications that came with their choice. The clean start they hoped for would not be as clean as they thought, because their lives would continue to be connected through their children. Ultimately they ignored the contributions their own dysfunction made to the problems of their marriage.

In difficult moments like these in our relationships we must remind ourselves that all marriages go through difficult seasons. A season is a span of time created by circumstances in our lives. Because we don't know how long a season will last we are tempted to project that difficult seasons will never come to an end. At some point in every marriage there comes a summer season that brings with it circumstances that feel like the dry, hot days of summer. Just like hot summers in Texas, the routine of life creates hot and dry conditions in our marriage.

These conditions cause us to look for relief as the routine of our life combines with a cycle of anticipation and disappointment, creating seemingly intolerable conditions in our relationship. We are lured to seek relief, to change our circumstances, and find a "relationally cooler" place. Strings of hurtful, insensitive responses between a husband and wife may add up like hundred-degree days in a hot Texas summer. In the same way we might be tempted to think summer will never end as the hot days of July drag on into August, we are tempted to conclude the situation in our marriage will never change. But summer does end. Just like summer changes into a cooler fall season, this season will change in your marriage too—if you will not give up your faithful efforts.

In addition to the "heat" brought about by the circumstances of our lives that push us to give up in discouragement, contestant thinking seeks to convince us of false dangers that lie ahead on the horizon of our marriage, like a mirage on a hot summer day. Imposing foreboding and imaginary doom on the horizon of our relationship as though they are real events an attempt to demand an immediate response. This sense of foreboding is heavy and may lead a husband or wife to act in urgency while responding to a phantom situation that has not materialized. A marriage is put into jeopardy when a hasty response is activated in an attempt to find relief. The uncomfortable heat in a summer season can act as a catalyst that provides energy for change in a marriage relationship. It can be a catalyst leading to positive change, carrying the couple on in pursuit of God's answers for the problems they face, or it can be a catalyst for negative change, pushing the marriage toward a risky, untimely choice.

The pressure of hot conditions can come into our relationship in a short blast—the result of a heated argument, the demands of a growing family, the pressures of a developing career, or a schedule that leads us to scramble our priorities. It really doesn't matter if it's a short blast or if it settles in as a full season of heat with a longer duration. The effects of the heat may produce short-term and long-term fatigue in a marriage relationship. The fatigue is magnified by the repeated cycles of anticipation and disappointment and begins to encompass all aspects of our relationship with its discomfort. A person may question or compromise the commitment they made to their spouse, and they may be tempted to throw caution to the wind in a risky attempt to create the relationship they desire.

The destructive forces arrayed against a marriage can present themselves like a perilous mirage with looming danger that demands a reaction. They encourage a person to pick one of the opportunities before them in order to avoid danger while promising the possibility of a lucky choice grand prize. The effort is to convince a person that danger is so imminent or things so intolerable that it is worth putting at risk all the treasure in life: relationships, reputation, finances, and most of all family.

Again, I have known many people who have chosen that path only to regret its hidden consequences a few years later. To share another story with you, many years ago when I walked into a restaurant for lunch, I noticed a friend I knew from church.

He was having lunch with a woman I didn't recognize, and I stepped over to the table to greet them. As I said hello, my friend responded awkwardly to me. He was formal in his response, introducing me as if we barely knew each other, though we had spent time together on several occasions. I greeted the lady he was with as he explained through our greeting that she was a consultant advising him on certain aspects of his business.

After a brief conversation that seemed to wash away the initial awkwardness, I excused myself to order and left them to finish their lunch. As I left the restaurant that day, I thought about the encounter and wondered why he had responded so awkwardly to me. I brushed aside the concerns that were running through my mind and calmed them with assurances that the awkwardness I felt was not due to something inappropriate going on between them. I knew him to be solidly committed to his marriage.

Several weeks went by before I received a call one night just as we were sitting down for dinner. It was from my friend, the one who I had seen in the restaurant, and by now the thoughts of our previous encounter had long been put to rest. He greeted me with a tone of seriousness in his voice and asked if we could talk. I said, "Sure, but can I call you back? We're about to sit down for dinner."

He said, "Oh, not tonight. I would like to talk with you in person. Could we meet for breakfast in the morning?"

I agreed to meet him, but before we set a place he wanted to know if our conversation would be kept confidential. Again his tone was serious, but I had no suspicions of what was on his mind. I told him I would keep whatever we discussed confidential but could not promise him it would be exclusive to just us. He asked why, and I said, "Because I am a man under authority, and you could tell me something that I might need to tell my boss or the authorities." I assured him that I cared for him and that anything he told me would be held to a small circle of people whose only interest would be to see God's wisdom and direction implemented in the decisions he was facing. He then informed me that if I could not assure him that the conversation would be held confidential between the two of us, he did not want to talk.

I was surprised by his response so I reiterated my assurance of confidentiality within a limited circle and added that I may not have to involve anyone else depending on the situation he wanted to discuss. I asked him to give me more details so that I could give him further assurances about the confidentiality he was requesting, but he wouldn't say anything more. We ended our conversation, leaving an uncomfortable tension between us without a time or place to meet. The next morning, instead of meeting with me, he met with his wife to tell her he had decided to leave her and their children for the woman I saw him with in the restaurant.

Jan and I were informed of his decision when his wife called in tears, devastated by the news that threw her life into complete chaos. Her husband had traded his reputation, relationships, finances, and family for what was behind Door #1, hoping luck would bring him the grand prize of marital bliss with another woman.

As the reality of his decision unfolded through the weeks and months following his phone call to me and then his communication with his wife, the impact of his decision became clear. His choice had brought destruction and devastation to his family. He moved away and deserted his family. Like many who have chosen door number one, his new life did not bring him the joy and perfect marriage he had hoped for, and his family struggled for many years trying to make sense of his shocking choices.

"Contestant thinking" leads individuals to trade something of great value for the possibility of something else that has eluded them without their having to work for it. Over half of all married couples in America have picked this door as the solution to the dissatisfaction and the brokenness of their marriage. The promise that the "wheeler-dealer" presents them offers them options in their mind that convinces them a greater prize, a better deal, lies right behind the door before them—all they need to do is make the trade.

DOOR NUMBER TWO: A COPING LIFE

For those who decline door number one, another opportunity waits to entice them. The "wheeler-dealer" isn't done. He continues to offer opportunities that test the boundaries of compromise in the circumstances of our marriages. An individual that has said no to door number one is holding on to what he has even if it may not be all he wants it to be because he is not willing to risk his reputation, relationships, finances, or the connection he has with his children for the promise of something better through starting over. That option puts too much at risk.

With door number one no longer an option, the "wheeler-dealer" offers door number two. Behind this door is compromise, withdrawal, and the status quo. Through the same cycle of anticipation and disappointment that developed "contestant thinking" in the first place, this couple continues their pursuit of "get rich quick" solutions to their problems. They are drawn to door number two by the lingering pain they feel from the cycles of anticipation and disappointment they've experienced in their marriage. Although they are not satisfied with their relationship, they have decided to stick with it but make no further efforts toward improving their relationship. The hurt from unmet expectations and disappointment is too great.

This door offers them the opportunity to sit down emotionally. Through the folded arms of inaction, they withdraw from their marriage relationship, refusing to engage anymore in a deep or relevant way with their partner. Their disappointment has produced such hurt that it has turned their interaction into escalating encounters of cynicism, invalidation, and rejection, leading them to conclude that withdrawal is their best option since they have said no to divorce.

I believe many couples choose this option as their door of solution. This means they have chosen to disengage from their marriages without divorcing their partner as the "solution" to their unhappiness. I have dealt with many unhappy men who have chosen this path. They feel stuck and unhappy, and they choose "coping" as their method of dealing with their unhappiness.

Maybe you know a couple like this. Perhaps even your own marriage has stopped growing and you are coping instead of growing in your relationship. Door number two locks up the pain of our relationship in a relational prison with no remedy and opens the door to a search for satisfying solutions to cope with our pain. The search can take many forms. It could be a hobby such as golfing, hunting, or fishing. It could be civic involvement or a community project that consumes all your time, focus, and attention. It may be increased time at work or with friends. The point is there is a need for distraction to get your mind off the situation. If a satisfying solution is not found discouragement, loneliness, and hopelessness settle in and create the need to medicate the pain just so coping can continue. Medicating the pain can take a dark, destructive path, creating other problems beyond the marriage. A decision to allow the marriage to remain "as is" leads to physical, emotional, or spiritual pain connected with settling for a relationship that can't or won't change because of the choice of one or both of the parties in the marriage.

It takes two equally committed individuals pouring all their efforts and their faith into the relationship for it to grow in connection and intimacy. When one or both parties have decided they must accept their relationship "as is"—being convinced nothing is going to change—they turn their attention toward hobbies, work interests, outside friendships, or even other more destructive behaviors that medicate their pain and enable them to continue in the brokenness of the relationship. But a life of brokenness is not what God intended for marriage, nor does it reflect the nature of His loving relationship with His church.

I want to pause here and say I am not ignoring the person who is alone in fighting for their marriage. It is possible for one individual in the marriage to embrace "contestant thinking" while the other remains engaged in their effort to build a partnership of connection and intimacy. When one person in the relationship seems to be willing to accept compromise while the other wants more from the relationship, it takes the one who is most engaged to tenaciously hold on for the change they desire to manifest.

That was the case in our marriage. One of the benefits of Jan's strong personality was the tenacity that she applied to our relationship. Her courage, commitment, and love, strengthened by her, grabbed ahold of me and held on. She kept her focus on God as He walked me to a place of awareness, change, and health for the benefit of our marriage.

My passive-aggressive approach to relational issues naturally lent itself to a path of compromise that would have put Jan and me on this road to coping with the frustrations and dissatisfaction we encountered on our way to the relational connection and intimacy we enjoy today. Denial and avoidance were willing partners, encouraging me to live in that folded-arm emotional withdrawal. Deep down I didn't want the fruit that compromise and coping would bring into our relationship, but I was ill equipped to make the necessary changes for a different result. I wanted deep connection and intimacy with this girl I loved, but I didn't know how to get there. Although we never embraced compromise as our solution to the unhappiness we experienced in our marriage, the pressure to choose compromise or develop coping mechanisms was present because of my passive-aggressive methods of relating.

what they have for ourselves. We mistakenly think the good things we see reflected in their lives are the result of luck or fate, and we resent the fact that they got lucky and we didn't. This thinking is based on a deceptive lie.

The truth is, God's blessings are available to all who desire them. However, they are distributed through our faith and obedience, which is reflected in our committed efforts to include God as we partner with our spouse to build our dream marriage. God is faithful to both redeem and restore all that we give to Him. It is not too late for you, no matter where you are in the circumstances of your life. Why don't you give him the brokenness of your life and the dissatisfaction you feel in your marriage and let Him bring healing, restoration, and wholeness to every area of your life?

Chapter 10

DRAMA QUEEN

❧ JAN ❧

S A GRANDMOTHER OF FIFTEEN PRECIOUS grandchildren, I am always amazed at how unique they all are. It is interesting to see the responses they each have to different situations. Some of them are born with natural confidence and boldness, and some are shy and don't want any attention on them. When we go out to a restaurant, it is interesting to see the difference in personalities show up when a parent asks his child to go ask the waiter for a refill on a drink. Most of the kids are too self-conscious to walk right up and ask for a refill, and no amount of coaxing is able to push them into it. But for a few of them, when you ask them to get their own refill, they look at you, smile, say OK, and walk right up to the counter and ask for what they want. I mean, some of my grandchildren are reduced to tears thinking they would have to perform this task, but to others it is no big deal. They are not embarrassed or reluctant. It is even fun for them. They aren't afraid of being told no or of being rejected, so it is not intimidating for them to walk right up and ask for what they want.

There is something innate inside that child that produces natural boldness and confidence that is not present in the other children. This bold approach to the situations of life is the mind-set of an assertive woman—somewhat fearless and not afraid to be told no. Her perspective is, "If you want something, ask for it. All they can say is no."

God's creation is full of such diversity, and the goal in marriage isn't to make everyone look the same. The goal is to figure out how we can make the confusing mess that is created by the difference in our personalities and perspectives into beautiful marriages. In order to do this, we have to be honest that we may unknowingly communicate with our spouses in a way that causes them to disconnect or shy away from us.

A Force to Reckon With

I grew up thinking that I should question things and that I shouldn't agree just for the sake of agreeing. This principle worked fine for me most of the time growing up, but in my marriage relationship it didn't work at all. My enthusiasm, coupled with my confident, opinionated nature sometimes caused Tom to emotionally shut down. I would be thinking that we were having a good time of tossing ideas back and forth, but Tom was thinking that I was being critical. I would be quick to notice something that needed to be done or something that needed to be changed and I would mention it to Tom, thinking that of course he would want to know, but to him I was being negative. If we want to engage our husbands in meaningful conversation, we have to be open to how we may unknowingly be sabotaging our communication with them. Our aggressive style may cause them to disconnect from us or make them want to emotionally retreat.

When does a strength that you rely on, even depend on, become a stumbling block for success and relational connection? How does a woman who is competent and bold embrace a style of communication that will not alienate her husband but instead draw him into partnership with her? A strong woman is usually bold and confident, not afraid to speak her mind because she is not afraid to be wrong—which doesn't happen very often! This confident mind-set, along with the ability to be brutally honest and a certain measure of insensitivity, becomes the very thing that causes unwanted friction in her marriage.

If you are an opinionated and assertive woman, you are likely prone to excel in most anything that you set your mind to. However, those attributes that contribute to your external success may also serve as a detriment in your marriage. Every strength has its weaknesses, and as intelligent women it would be wise for us to recognize our weaknesses and how they affect the ones that we love most.

Differences in communication style and strength of personality can lead to misunderstandings and disconnection with our spouses. In this chapter we will discuss how an assertive woman can use her strengths as relational assets to strengthen the bond of connection and avert the disconnection with her husband that can be produced by her assertive ways. No matter where you are in your relationship—just beginning or married a long time—connection takes focus of attention and work.

THE SUZIE INCIDENT

Tom and I had been dating for a few months and as sixteen-year-olds had decided we weren't going to see other people but would be "going steady." Of course as juniors in high school we didn't have a huge social life anyway, but we had decided to have an exclusive dating relationship.

Then one day I was talking to one of my friends on the phone and she mentioned that Tom had called another friend whom I'll call Suzie and asked what she thought about girls wearing eye makeup. Tom and Suzie were friends, but he and I were going steady, so it caught me off guard. I said, "What? He called Suzie on the phone and talked to her about eye makeup?" He had never even talked to me about eye makeup!

I hung up with my friend and called Tom immediately. I was in shock and was sure this was a mistake. I mean, we talked to other people at school and stuff, but I never talked to another guy on the phone, and I thought he didn't either.

I asked Tom if it was true, and he stammered around a little and then said it was. He and Suzie were good friends, and he didn't think there was anything wrong with talking to her on the phone. Well, I started crying and could hardly talk. He was in shock and didn't know what to do. He really didn't understand where I was coming from, and that made me more upset. So he began to apologize over and over, but he just didn't see that he did anything wrong. I could tell he didn't get how I felt, and that made it worse. I was thinking maybe our relationship wasn't what I had thought it was.

I don't remember all that was said—just that there was lots of crying. Tom was trying to make me feel better and just wanted to know what he could do to make it up. I had no idea. I was hurt and had not even thought of coming up with a solution. So he said to me, "Would you like it if I never talked to Suzie again?"

That got my attention.

He said, "If it would make you feel better, I will never talk to Suzie again."

Well, that calmed me down and sounded like a great solution, so I said OK. I felt better—only I didn't realize he meant he would never talk to her again *at all*. I thought we were addressing the issue of calling other girls, and he was addressing the issue of talking to Suzie. So he told her at school the next day they couldn't ever talk again because it upset me. She fell apart, and I didn't even realize what was going on until my friend told me what Tom had said and how Suzie had responded.

Well, I was mortified at the turn of events, and when I finally was able to talk to Tom, I asked him what in the heck he was doing. He told me he was living true to his word. He had said he would never talk to her again, and he was proving to me he never would.

I said, "But this is not what I wanted. I just don't want you to call other girls without telling me about it."

But he had made up his mind that talking to Suzie was the problem, and he kept his word. It was quite the talk among our friends. Tom's solution to my emotional outburst was to make an all-or-nothing response. It was his way of calming my emotions and demonstrating his commitment to me. Ultimately, it was not satisfying to me. I felt totally misunderstood and confused, but the damage was done. Our friends thought I was being ridiculous, and Suzie never spoke to me again.

This is an example of the many ways we miscommunicated that carried right into our marriage. Neither one of us was pleased with the outcome of our conversation.

It Takes Talking

Our communication styles were totally different right from the beginning of our relationship. We were young, and we had no idea how to handle it. We just knew we liked each other and wanted to be a couple, so we built coping mechanisms around the things that didn't work. We were slow to understand and appreciate each other's differences and even slower in learning how to relate in a meaningful way. Because we didn't learn this when we were dating, it has required a lot of work and gracious understanding in our marriage.

I think a lot of couples share this problem. We are left in a fog when our communication goes awry, and we try to put the pieces back together after the damage has been done. We haven't yet come to appreciate and understand the differences in our communication styles, so cycles of disconnection are continued.

The only way to have true intimacy in a marriage is through open, honest communication. We cannot assume we know or understand what our spouse is thinking unless we have a verbal conversation with them about it. We have to communicate our thoughts to each other to be able to honestly relate.

Many conflicts in our marriage have occurred because of what we thought the other person was saying or thinking, not because of their actual words. Even if you know your spouse very well, it is possible to misinterpret or misunderstand something they have said. To have effective communication, you have to be a good listener as well as a good talker. Good listening involves having an open mind to hear their perspective and then having a back-and-forth dialogue with your spouse about the issue.

charge! Understanding and respect for the other person and their perspective is the foundation for healthy communication. Even though I am aware of the importance of that foundation, it flies out the window in the face of feeling ignored.

I'm appalled to think of all the times I got mad at Tom for what he was saying because of how I interpreted it. At the time all I could hear was how it made me feel and I was not able to see what he intended. The way he processes information and reacts to situations is so different than the way I process and react to them, and he usually does things differently than I would. It would frustrate me to no end that he couldn't see things the way I did. The difference in his approach felt disrespectful to mine, and with the red cape waving I would charge into a conversation about our differences.

Sometimes we get so caught up in our own perspective of things that we can't even hear or acknowledge our spouse's perspective. It can be annoying when you have a way you want them to see things and they just don't get it—even after you have explained it many times. It is especially frustrating when you think you are right and they are wrong. But at that point— at the point when your passion is strong and there is a forward-charging momentum in the conversation that would cause you to force what you want—it is imperative that you stop, take a break, and listen to your husband without demeaning or diminishing him for not being on the same page as you. It takes a huge effort to stop and listen to the person you think is wrong and with a good attitude make a diligent attempt to understand their perspective. But if we want to have a healthy satisfying relationship, we have to value their different perspective as much as our own as we seek to learn what does and does not work in our communication. We must let our spouse know we are committed to working on our problems and finding a mutually satisfying solution as we seek to learn what does and does not work in our communication.

TAKE A TIME-OUT

A tool for resolving conflict that Tom and I have learned to apply when we are struggling to communicate clearly is to take a time-out. By that I mean stopping the conversation if it becomes too heated. One of us can call a time-out if we feel we need time to cool off and regroup. It is a protection you establish that will help you when conflict arises. But it needs to be established before a conflict develops because in the heat of the conflict you will most likely lose the ability to have a rational discussion about how you want to proceed in resolving the conflict. The agreement you make needs to state that if you need time to cool off, you can call a time-out without being penalized. It is important to make sure that you both agree that it is only for a specific time period and after that you reconnect again in an effort to resolve the conflict.

It is up to the two of you to determine the length of time it takes to cool down and get a clear head—it might be thirty minutes, an hour, two hours, or even a day. During the break you can think and pray about what is going on and work to identify the problem apart from the emotions surrounding the conflict. Then at the agreed time, you come back together and continue the discussion from the perspective that you are working on this issue together to come to a mutually satisfying agreement.

By agreeing in advance about taking a time-out, you cut off the chance for offense and rejection that can happen in the heat of the argument if you stomp out of the room or leave the house and drive around for an hour while you think and cool off. It produces a calm in the middle of a storm. The goal is to come back with a different mind-set of being partners working on a solution rather than opponents in a competition.

Also, do not think that giving the silent treatment is the same as verbally saying you need a time-out and want to reconnect. Walking away without communicating and withdrawing without communicating are not the best ways to cool off from a heated disagreement. Both of these acts can be punitive and meant to hurt the other person. If it happens regularly it can become toxic in its effect on the relationship. What we are trying to do is keep the negative damage that results from arguing to a minimum by laying a foundation of trust and respect through putting protective plans in place.

If you need to take a time-out to cool off, that is fair and effective—sometimes even necessary! But it is important to have a firm commitment that you will not use the time-out as an excuse to withdraw with the intention to hurt and reject each other. Your commitment must be firm and demonstrated in the moment that you will honestly use the time-out to calm yourselves and identify the issues of your frustration. In other words, you need to fight fairly—even when everything in you wants to hurt and reject the other person. This is why it is important to talk in advance about ways you will stay connected to the process of resolving conflict.

Check the Drama

Aggressive women are often decisive, and maybe a little demanding. Part of the dynamic between passion and passive is that strong, passionate women are usually full speed ahead in a conversation while the passive husband is left in the dust, trying to figure out what we are saying and what he really thinks about it. We may feel justified in running over him in a conversation because we don't appreciate or think we have time to wait for his response. We have a result we want or need to have happen, and we think that if he can't get on board with us, we will just blow right by him to get a result. Through our charging approach to the conversation, we have sabotaged the connection and partnership we desire with him. And through experience, they have learned that if we are full speed ahead, they probably won't be listened to anyway so they don't feel motivated to engage in the process. We are left feeling alone when what we wanted was partnership, agreement, and connection.

This whole dynamic develops some unhealthy habits in our communication style that need to be addressed and changed. Unhealthy communication habits lead us to build coping mechanisms to deal with the anger and frustration we experience in unresolved conflict. Instead of taking a good look at our frustration and agreeing that it is a reflection that something is broken and needs to be fixed, we carry on with our normal approach to get our way regardless of the cost. This unhealthy dynamic robs us of the growth and deepening intimacy we want and need in the relationship.

The passionate personality creates drama wherever it goes. That can be great and fun if there is no conflict involved. But when passion creates drama that leads to conflict, things become irrational. Drama enhances the emotions and intensity of words beyond what is rational or reasonable. And yet when you have a dramatic personality, you are feeling things intensely and it is natural to just let your communication go there. It feels as if your emotions are true and real, so you can't

tick as he tried to remember a time when he *did* give me flowers for no reason. It may have only been once, but because I said *never*, he would process my point as invalid because of my misstatement.

Tom would get stuck on the extravagance of my expression or the strength of my terms and totally miss what I was trying to express through my passion. He would then begin to debate the legitimacy of my expression as he pointed out exceptions to the strong statements I had made. This was like throwing gasoline on the fire of my passion. My passion over the issue split in two. I now had anger toward him about this along with the passion I had over the first issue. As we talked, I had to defend what I was saying while trying to communicate the issue in a way that "tamped down" the strength of my feelings so it could get by the "watchdog" of his memory processor. This was an ugly, ineffective process that caused me the hurt feelings of being misunderstood, invalidated, and rejected.

Tom has come to realize it isn't the words he should be listening to, as they are the vehicle that carries my pain. What I need in that moment is not a debate over the validity of my perspective. I need him to sympathize with me as I process my pain!

Through all this, we have to make a firm commitment to hang in there as we're learning the things that work and don't work in our communication styles. Because we are committed, we are actively trying to stay connected with each other through the process of unraveling the knots we have made in our relationship and then learning to connect in a healthy, balanced way.

Let's Talk About You

Have you seen yourself in this chapter? Maybe you have been wondering, "What can I do to better manage and express my frustration? How can I get my husband to engage in dialog with me?" A good place to start is to recognize the destructive thoughts and actions you are doing to tear down your relationship. Refuse to let the drama of your feelings and hurts have a louder voice than the needs and wishes of your husband. Tell yourself this is not a time to walk away in anger and frustration. Ask the Lord to help you calm down and be respectful as you work to listen and discover what might be your part in the problem.

I know from my own experience that when the smoke of all that effort clears, the destructive side of the Drama Queen will be gone and you will be left with the good, fun side of the personality God has given you. Who knows? You may even give the term *Drama Queen* a good name!

Chapter 11

FINDING RESOLUTION

❧ JAN ❧

HEN OUR KIDS WERE YOUNG, WE WOULD occasionally go out of town for a weekend alone. On one of these trips we left the kids with a sitter and drove to Lubbock, Texas, from Amarillo, Texas, for a little getaway. We had a great time and were all packed up—ready to go back home. Tom pulled out of the parking lot of the motel and turned onto the highway and started driving toward the Loop. (If you live in Lubbock, you know what the Loop is—no other description is necessary!)

He said to me, "I am going this way because I know this is the way you would want to go."

I asked, "What do you mean it's the way I would want to go?"

He replied, "I would go home a different way, but I am preferring you, so I am going this way."

Mildly annoyed, I responded, "Well, what way would you go?"

He told me the way he was thinking, and I continued, "Well, that way would take longer, so of course you would go this way. It only makes sense. It isn't preferring me. It is just going the best way home."

That irritated Tom and he said, "No, I'm preferring you."

To which I replied, "No, it's the fastest way."

I got out a map and showed him the error of his ways. (This was long before Google maps!) He was not persuaded and said he would take the extra hour it would take to get home in order to drive both ways to see which one was shortest.

We were coming off a great weekend together and barely moved out of the parking lot before we were both mad at each other! The connection we felt over the weekend and had nurtured during our time away quickly evaporated into conflict. I talked him out of trying both ways and then we didn't talk to each other again for an hour, both of us fuming because we weren't being understood. Tom's comment was taken way out of proportion by me, but I was frustrated he had concluded that what he was doing was preferring me without even talking to me.

Of course, Tom was not trying to start an argument when he initiated the conversation. He was pointing out that he was doing something intentionally nice for me. But it hit me the wrong way. I reacted to his words and more intensely to his motive. "Why would I would want him to take a long way home?" I thought. "He obviously doesn't even know what I prefer. But he thinks he does. What a jerk." I'm sure he was thinking, "This conversation is not going the way I intended it to go in my head!"

The conversation ended up in a ridiculous place. But don't judge me—you know you have been there. Most of our disagreements are about small, insignificant things, but little things become big things when we have communication problems. Issues that are simmering under the surface are just waiting to bubble over, to scorch us, and to bring division between us.

Effort Is Key

We all desire to have a good relationship with our spouse. That is why we took vows and married them: to have a lifelong partnership. But the reality of trying to stay connected in a busy, distracted world is difficult. It takes intentional commitment by partners who are willing to look at the problems in their relationship and to stay connected while they work out their issues.

It is amazing how quickly issues can escalate into an argument. If you have been married for any length of time, you know that some of the grace you had for your differences when you were dating begin to wear off as the reality of the work of marriage sets in. What you may have ignored or easily forgiven when you were dating can become what seems to be an irreconcilable difference as your married life goes on.

This kind of argument we had when leaving Lubbock sounds like the kind of thing you would hear two cranky old people talking about. But we were not old—we were just not communicating well. Our argument may seem trivial to you, but twenty-five years later I can still remember it vividly. We never should have reacted to each other the way we did, especially over something so unimportant. But isn't that the way these kind of conversations go? We don't start out with the intent to have an argument. We are trying to connect to each other, just going along, sharing with each other, and all of a sudden there is a bump. Then another bump. Then a *thump, thump, thump,* and all of a sudden we are stranded on the highway of life with a flat tire, needing help.

Misunderstandings cause friction, pain, and anger if they are not addressed. Things that should not be a problem seem to become insurmountable mountains in our lives. Misunderstandings and miscommunications can bring about the most ridiculous conversations you can imagine, but most of the time we are halfway up the mountain before we realize we're in trouble. It takes time and effort to unravel these discussions, and both people have to stay engaged in the process. Connection will happen when we don't reject each other's communication style and we make allowances for their differences by being willing to speak each other's language.

I'm regretful to think of all the times I became mad at Tom for what he was saying because of how I interpreted it. At the time all I could think was how it made me feel, and I was not able to see what he intended. In marriage we have to make a firm commitment to hang in there through the process of unraveling the knots we have made and then unravel them together to reconnect to our spouse. We cannot let the drama of our feelings and hurts have a louder voice than the needs and wishes of our spouse. Because we are committed to having a good marriage, we are actively trying to stay connected with each other and trying to stop the destructive thoughts and actions that tear down the relationship. We need to calm down and be respectful and listen to discover what might be our part in the problem.

Again, taking time-out to cool off can be important. This is not a time to walk away in anger and frustration. If you need to process the discussion, it is important to clearly communicate that the break in conversation is for a specific time and that you will reconnect again after a given time period of cooling off and reflection. I touched on this in the last chapter, but I feel like it is good to reiterate: taking a time-out when discussions are heated is a really effective strategy if done correctly. As long as you communicate that you are taking a time-out and will come back when you've calmed down to resolve the conflict, it is a really helpful way to allow emotions to settle and avoid hurtful words sometimes spoken in a heated moment. By deciding upon a strategy ahead of time, you can easily use this strategy when you need it. What we are trying to do is keep the negative damage caused by arguing from hurting the relationship by laying a foundation of trust and respect.

Know That It Matters

∽ Tom ∾

Unresolved conflict doesn't just evaporate. It gets stored in our subconscious and becomes compressed with other unresolved conflict, acting like the gunpowder in a shotgun shell. It is waiting to be hit by a trigger to initiate the explosion. Layer upon layer of unresolved conflict festers in our subconscious, becoming unstable over time as it awaits a trigger event. When the trigger event happens, it causes an explosion that at the least brings things to a halt between us while the cause of the explosion is being addressed but it has the potential to cause serious emotional hurt, damaging the relationship. The damage becomes much greater because of the accumulation of unresolved events. It could have been lessened if we would have addressed and resolved the issues at the time they happened.

Should our goal be to eliminate conflict in our relationship? If conflict was eliminated, would the road be paved for our deepest and best connection in marriage? Every relationship experiences conflict. Our expectation is not to eliminate conflict but to develop methods of responding to conflict in a timely way that produces healing, forgiveness, reconciliation, and the fruitful connection we desire in our relationship. We're going to share some of what we've learned about this with you.

Sometimes It Takes Time

As we drove home from the event Jan just shared of the momentous miscommunication event in our marriage, I thought about my response to Jan and wanted to make it right, but I didn't know how. I had been having an internal conversation since our getaway began because Jan had made a comment in a conversation we were having that I never did things the way she wanted. I should have asked what she meant by that instead of having an internal dialogue with myself (again!). That would have opened the door to the discussion of her feelings and given me the chance to express what I was feeling in response to her comment. But my internal processing of the offhand comment she made earlier in our trip produced the strength of my aggressive, stubborn response to her when we left the hotel and I tried to point out that I was preferring her. Instead of earning credit with Jan, I ended up causing the hurt we then had to reconcile.

The first thing I want to say is that passive-aggressive thinking causes a fog that makes understanding the motive behind conflict difficult to fully identify. As we drove home, after a long period of silence, I finally addressed her with the only appropriate thing I could say: "I am sorry."

"I am sorry, babe," I said. "I am sorry for my stubborn response to you and for the hurt I caused by caring more about being right than I did about your feelings."

We then began to open up to each other and uncover all that was involved in creating the whole incident that had just happened. Why did it take me so long to make that move toward resolving our conflict? Why couldn't I just say I was sorry sooner?

With the years of healing that now allow me to better recognize my method of relating in situations of conflict, I can say the reason it took so long was because of the internal processing of passive-aggressive thinking that clouded my perspective. My clouded thinking provided the structure for pride, anger, and stubbornness to create a barrier between us that had to be overcome through my response. My response could not just be the words, "I'm sorry." It had to represent a heartfelt understanding of the hurt I caused, and my passive-aggressive way of relating created a fog that took me a while to clear. My eventual apology in words and attitude opened the door for deeper conversation that led to healing and forgiveness over that event, but it remains today as an epic moment of conflict in our marriage.

Put the Marriage First

This conflict between Jan and me is an example of how the most unbelievable and insignificant things change from molehill to a mountain when we determine that we will defend our perspective without regard to the damage it may cause to the marriage. But Dr. John Gottman, a professor of psychology at the University of Washington and the author of several best-selling books on marriage, warns us against this. In his book *The Seven Principles for Making Marriage Work*, he states:

> In the strongest marriages, husband and wife share a deep sense of meaning. They don't just "get along"—they

also support each other's hopes and aspirations and build a sense of purpose into their lives together. That is what I mean when I talk about honoring and respecting each other. Very often a marriage's failure to do this is what causes husband and wife to find themselves in endless, useless rounds of argument or to feel isolated and lonely in their marriage. After watching countless videotapes of couples fighting, I can guarantee you that most quarrels are really not about whether the toilet lid is up or down or whose turn it is take out the trash. There are deeper, hidden issues that fuel these superficial conflicts and make them far more intense and hurtful than they would otherwise be.[1]

You may have experienced this firsthand in your own marriage as a series of silly, insignificant, disagreements mushroomed out of control into a barrier that changed your perspective and then ultimately led to a change in the commitment you made to your marriage. The focus on one situation or the explosion that results from multiple unresolved conflicts in the relationship changed your behavior and positioned you to defend something ridiculous while sacrificing the thing or person you held most precious. It is a sad fact that the most common reason given to the court in a petition of divorce is *irreconcilable differences*. Rather than tell the judge the little things that started the process that led to this point of making the decision to end the relationship, we simply state it can't be worked out.

I do not mean to minimize the pain associated with divorce or to belittle a process that brings a couple to such a monumental decision. As a pastor, I am well aware of the pain and suffering associated with divorce for all those involved. The intent is not to question the process that led you where you are

THE FAITH FACTOR

When Jan and I entered into our marriage, we each had individual relationships with God and a commitment to pursue and serve Him. That made involving Him in our relationship an easy and natural step. That foundation gave us a spiritual perspective on things that influenced and impacted our relationship. Our faith supports our commitment to each other and serves to motivate our efforts to resolve conflict by giving us perspective on problems that may seem overwhelming. At strategic moments we remind each other that the size of our problem is not bigger than God's ability to work on our behalf. That helps us to carry on through the discouragement of the moment. Also, our faith gives us a greater perspective than the problem we are currently facing by reminding us of the abundance of blessings, fruitfulness, and happiness in our relationship. Keeping a proper perspective during conflict helps us combat hopelessness when it tries to settle upon us as we work to resolve the conflict. Through a personal commitment to God, our faith provides a foundation for the work required to build and maintain a happy and healthy relationship.

USE YOUR WORDS WISELY

All problem-solving begins with communication. It's not just the quantity of words we use that's important as we discuss the situation of conflict; it's also the quality of words we use to describe what we are feeling. In their book *Fighting for Your Marriage* Howard Markman, Scott Stanley, and Susan Blumberg identify destructive patterns of communication that become toxic as they prevent conflict resolution and greatly increase the risk of unhappiness and divorce. The four patterns they identify are 1) escalation, 2) invalidation, 3) withdrawal and avoidance, and 4) negative interpretations. These patterns are progressive in their impact as couples attempt to resolve conflict and establish connection with each other.[4]

Conflict can escalate as we associate past events, other frustrations, and hurts with the current issue of conflict. It escalates through the verbal dogpile that takes place as we add other items to the discussion surrounding the event that has become our focus. Escalation makes everything fair game in our conversation, leading us to intense, heated debate.

Furthermore, we invalidate our partner using a variety of methods when we subtly or directly put down their thoughts, feelings, or character in our communication. We invalidate them as we minimize their input or contribution to the relationship. Our nonverbal communication can be just as invalidating, such as rolling our eyes, grunting, sighing, or ignoring them altogether. When these patterns of communication are established in the relationship, they produce withdrawal and avoidance, which can open the door to all kinds of negative interpretations.

Realizing how our words nurture or destroy, Jan and I made an agreement as we entered marriage never to undermine our commitment to each other in our communication. It is so easy in the heat and frustration associated with a conflict to insert statements that undermine the commitment we have made to each other, such as. "Maybe we never should have gotten married," "You would be happier with someone else," or "Maybe we should just get a divorce." Throughout all the years of our marriage, no matter what the level of frustration, disappointment, or conflict we have faced, we have not used words with each other that undermined our commitment to each other and to our marriage vows.

PLAY FAIR WITH APOLOGIES

Our efforts to guard our words as we communicate are necessary, but they must be supported by our willingness to own our mistakes. It seems simple to say that we need to apologize to each other, but often that is easier said than done.

The "no apology" apology

An apology must clearly describe what we are sorry for, rather than being a blanket statement designed to produce peace, such as, "If I have done anything to offend you, I am sorry." That is an apology that is "no apology," as we call it in our marriage. Jan would not stand for the "no apology" apology in our marriage. I wanted to avoid conflict and create peace so, early on I often tried the "no apology" method of apologizing to resolve conflict. It was my quick effort to regain peace and connection when we had experienced conflict. However, she wouldn't let me get away with it. She always asked me what I was sorry for, and if I couldn't tell her specifically what I was sorry for, it was considered a "no apology" and was not accepted. A "no apology" is an attempt to cover up your mistake without repairing the damage. The apology is not reflective of a repentant heart if you can't put in to words specifically what was done that caused the hurt and needs to be repaired.

The "motive excuse"

The second barrier to an apology is the "motive excuse." The motive excuse prevents an apology from happening because the person holds to the fact that the hurt wasn't intentional. I began to realize that part of my defensive response to Jan related to the motive behind my action, not the action itself. Jan would confront me on what I had done, and my response was to defend the intent of my actions rather than own their results. My response to her confronting me with something I did would be to say, "No, I didn't." But being quite confident in the facts of what my behavior had produced in her, she would say, "Yes, you did." And around we would go. The facts related to the situation were indisputable, but since they didn't reflect the intent of my action, in my mind my pure motive excused the action and became the basis of my defense.

The "motive excuse" is stealthy. I didn't recognize it easily or quickly, and so it often became a barrier in our efforts to resolve conflict and for me to sincerely say I was sorry. It inserts a completely different, almost unrelated perspective into the conversation. Without acknowledging the validity of the facts, it defends and denies the actions that caused the conflict. The strength of my defense was based on my belief that Jan was saying I intended to do the stupid thing that hurt her or ignored her or disrespected her or whatever else I had done. I couldn't own to that because I never intended to hurt her.

Of course, all this was not as clear to me then as it is now. My feelings and Jan's facts clouded our ability to identify exactly what was taking place at the time. Jan needed me to acknowledge the impact of my behavior on her, and I wanted her to acknowledge that what resulted was not my intention. Those two conversations never connected on their own. The "motive excuse" polarizes our perspectives so that we talk to each other from opposite directions. That process will not get us to a place of apologizing for what we have done.

It helps me to avoid the "motive excuse" barrier when being confronted by Jan if she begins the conversation with, "I don't think you meant it this way, but...," and then tells me the impact of my actions on her. I can more easily take responsibility and apologize for my action if I know that she understands my motive was different than the result my flawed action produced.

The "you were wrong too" blame game

Another excuse for not apologizing is the "what they did was worse than what I did" excuse. It flows right into the "they made me do it" excuse. If the other person doesn't apologize for their part, we tell ourselves we don't have to apologize for ours. And even if they *do* apologize, we think they really needed to apologize because their action was so egregious—whereas we shouldn't have to apologize because we were only reacting to them.

It sort of sounds like double talk, doesn't it? And it is! This type of pride prevents us from humbly accepting what's happened and giving an apology. We are more interested in the issue than the relationship. It is dishonest and deceptive and needs to be recognized as a relationship destroyer. Good communication that leads us to a sincere apology paves the way for forgiveness and reconnection in our relationship. Forgiveness and reconnection are the ultimate goal we seek as we process through conflict to a peaceful resolution.

ASPIRE TO RECONCILE

Reconciliation is a process that enables us to see a situation and the results it has produced in the same way our spouse sees it. As we work through the issues that have caused us hurt and frustration, our goal is the same as reconciling our bank statement. In that process the statement is not reconciled until our check register and the bank statement say the same thing regarding the financial balance in the account. When we seek relational reconciliation, we must discuss the "charges" against us and the "withdrawals" made against the relationship and bring them to the place where they say the same thing. That involves a process.

When we have been wronged, an injustice has been created. Our choice is either to seek to establish our own justice for wrongs done to us or to give up that right and trust God to bring about justice on our behalf. God is just, and He promises to resolve every injustice (Rom. 12:19). Forgiveness is a choice we make to give up our right to extract a penalty for what was done to us. Unforgiveness holds on to that right and tries to extract the penalty using any means available to us. If we are going to live in the forgiveness that has been provided to us through Jesus Christ, then we must extend forgiveness to those who have wronged us (Matt. 6:12).

Some of the injustice done to us has caused such great pain that the thought of giving up the right to demand a penalty seems like an impossible task. I get that. It is not impossible, but it does take faith. It is a clear demonstration of our confidence that God will bring about the appropriate justice for our injustice.

Are you waiting for justice to be served before you make the decision to forgive? Are you directly or indirectly seeking to extract your own type of "vigilante" justice rather than trusting God to bring about the justice that is needed? You will not produce reconciliation in your relationship without forgiveness.

One of the most consistent traits that has been demonstrated through Jan's life has been forgiveness, and I have been the beneficiary. Through many of the accounts shared in this book, you have been made aware of the silly, selfish, stupid things I have done that have caused Jan hurt. Yet she has lived her faith and actively chosen not to extract her own penalty in our relationship. She has determined to trust God with the hurt and injustice it created and to live her life in the freedom that forgiveness supplies. That left me with the choice to walk in the freedom that she and God extended to me in our relationship and to work to rebuild trust that had been broken through my actions.

A decision to forgive is a decision not to extract your own justice, but that does not preclude a need to rebuild trust. Often this step in the reconciliation process is misunderstood or ignored. We must be aware that when there has been an injustice, it has created a breach of trust in the relationship. Once trust has been broken, it has to be re-earned. That is how a person is described as trustworthy or untrustworthy. Many times when dealing with an issue that has caused hurt and produced an injustice, a couple thinks only of the need or responsibility to forgive but ignores the process needed to reestablish trust.

In a relationship where there have been multiple hurts and injustices inflicted through the words and behavior of one person, there can develop such a breach of trust that although forgiveness is extended, the relationship can't be reconciled because the individual is untrustworthy and unwilling to do the work required to rebuild the trust. Establishing boundaries for accountability is not a reflection of unforgiveness but is the support system that protects the work required to reconstruct trust in the relationship on the way to reconciliation.

Let's Talk About You

As we bring this chapter to a close, I hope it has become clear that good communication in a relationship is essential. Jan and I have learned through many situations what things work and do not work for us. It is our prayer that as you read this, God begins to show you areas in your relationship where you can grow in your communication and openness with your spouse. If there have been areas of past hurt, we encourage you to take time to come to a place where you are walking in complete forgiveness toward each other. Receive outside counseling when needed. And if there are areas where trust needs to be rebuilt, it is worth taking the steps toward that end.

Whenever there is tension in your marriage, let us recommend to you that rather than going down the paths of invalidation, withdrawal, or excuses, you find a healthy resolution. As you purpose in your marriage to bring all conflict through to healthy resolution, you will find much more fulfillment and satisfaction in your relationship. All relationships have conflict, but there is a godly way to let conflict bring you closer together rather than push you further apart. Go with God's ways of communicating, extending forgiveness, and rebuilding trust, and then stand back and watch His miraculous work in your lives!

Chapter 12

THE POWER OF CONNECTION

⤜⤏ TOM ⤜⤏

AN AND I HAVE EXPERIENCED DISCONNECTION in our relationship over the years in small things and big things. We recognize that relational disconnection happens to some degree in all marriages. The more we understand and embrace each layer of connection, though, the deeper and more satisfying the connection in our marriage will be. So in this chapter we're going to talk about those layers of connection and how to strengthen each one.

I'll begin by saying it takes communication, honesty, and diligent effort to establish and maintain a connection with your spouse. Like the wireless connection on your computer or smartphone, it takes a properly working process for connection to happen. When it is working—when you have connection—your relationship hums along nicely. When it is not working, the feelings of disconnection are as frustrating and disorienting as when your computer Wi-Fi connection isn't working. You know what I mean? Panic sets in. Often you have to call in a professional to fix the problem.

Having a relational connection is not like a program we can run or a few settings we can adjust to make everything suddenly work smoothly. It involves a process in our hearts. You may think that connection should just happen naturally, and sometimes it does. But often connecting involves a process of learning, communicating, and growing with each other.

This is because concepts were formed in us while we were growing up that now affect our behavior as adults, and therefore they affect our interaction in marriage. It is important to recognize the influences that have shaped our lives. I came into marriage with a certain idea of the roles that a husband and a wife were to play in their relationship. My understanding was shaped by many influences—from sources such as my parents, my grandparents, my friends' families, and romantic concepts of love and relationships depicted in movies, music, and books. Many of the influences in my life were good and healthy, but some were not, and the picture they created of the roles and responsibilities in marriage was incomplete and inaccurate. I had to uncover the unhealthy ideas I had about marriage and make necessary adjustments as I grew in my marriage relationship with Jan.

For the fullest and deepest connection to develop, we must be willing to at least consider that our current view is flawed and be willing to embrace a new view of our responsibilities in marriage. Maybe you have never thought of the connection with your spouse in the way we are addressing it here. Sometimes couples wonder, "If connection requires this much thought and effort, is our relationship really motivated by love? I mean, if we love each other, shouldn't it be easy and natural to stay connected? It seems so mechanical. Maybe I married the wrong person. Staying connected wasn't hard when we were dating, so why should it be hard now that we're married?"

My short explanation is this: connection was not the focus of your relationship while you were dating. It was the by-product of the way you related with each other. If a couple does not sense a connection in the early stages of their dating relationship, their relationship ends because one or both people conclude they're not compatible, and they move on. However, once two people are married, intimacy becomes an important focus in the process of developing and maintaining fulfillment and satisfaction in the relationship. When that connection becomes blocked in some way, it doesn't help to point fingers of blame at each other or to deny that things are out of sync. It takes sensitivity, cooperation, and hard work to identify and overcome the barrier to the connection.

As Jan and I began our marriage, it was surprising to me that connecting with her was not an easy process. We had an active, spiritual, affectionate dating relationship. It was fun and easy for us to connect then, so I thought our connection in marriage would be easier, deeper, and stronger and would happen with little effort. What I found was that the easy, fun, and natural connection we wanted took a lot more work to achieve in marriage.

When I think of the relational connection that's possible in marriage, I think of a process that involves three general categories: physical connection, emotional connection, and spiritual connection. The deepest level of intimacy is achieved when we have developed connection in all three categories. Let's look at each one.

Bonding Through Physical Connection

I came into marriage with the idea that our physical connection was the most important connection in our marriage relationship. I thought any other kind of connection we shared would be the by-product of a satisfying sexual relationship between us. My solution to feeling any disconnection from Jan involved having more frequent sex. I was sure that all other areas of our life would be made better and more complete when we had sex more often. As time went on, I began to realize that the connection we desired didn't deepen as the result of more frequent sex. It was not the fix-all solution for disconnection in our relationship that I thought. The reality is that sexual intimacy alone does not produce relational connection.

I have talked to couples who are very sexually active yet feel totally disconnected in their relationships. Their sexual frequency and passion does not necessarily lead them to an overall satisfying connection in their marriage. I found in our marriage that a satisfying physical connection is greatly enhanced when emotional and spiritual connections are established. It does not hold true that a satisfying physical connection will necessarily produce emotional and spiritual connection. The more connection we experience in all three categories of connection—physical, emotional, and spiritual—the deeper and richer will be the love and satisfaction in our relationship.

God established sex to be enjoyable and satisfying in the context of a loving, committed marriage relationship. But we know that many couples enter into marriage with sexual experiences that have hurt them and have had a negative influence on their ability to respond sexually to their spouse. When sexual abuse, sexual trauma, sexual addictions, or promiscuity have been part of your life, the impact from those experiences will affect your marriage and may make it difficult to establish a healthy relationship with your spouse.

The hurts from these issues may be years in your past, yet they continue to impact you today. These issues need to be brought to a place of healing and wholeness for a healthy connection to take place. Left unaddressed, the hurtful experiences will remain a barrier against connecting with your spouse in a deep and mutually satisfying way.

If your physical connection is hindered by experiences from your past, there are many good resources available to you. I have listed several in the appendix at the back of this book. They can serve as a source of help for you as you ask God to bring healing and freedom to your life. In addition to these resources I would encourage you to seek a qualified counselor to help you address these issues.

Sometimes the culprit of disconnection is simply busyness and the demands of family. It makes the effort to connect too draining.

No matter the reason for disconnection in your relationship, the remedy is to admit that you are disconnected and to intentionally focus on and prioritize connecting with your spouse. By giving your spouse quality time, you further the opportunity for the connection you desire. As I look back over our married life, I can see the times that disconnection affected our marriage. God, as our loving partner, has helped us identify points of disconnection. This enabled us to work together to overcome these issues and to finally develop the relationship we desire with each other.

Relating Through Emotional Connection

～ Jan ～

The hardest thing Tom and I have had to deal with in our marriage happened a few years ago. There came an issue between us that we absolutely could not agree on. We had never dealt with this kind of block to our communication in all the years of our marriage. It started with each of us giving our own perspective about the issue we were dealing with. As we talked, we disagreed with each other, and we tried to persuade the other to see it our way. We kept presenting our own perspective, but we couldn't agree with the other's perspective. We kept talking and arguing. We tried adding more words as we attempted to come to an agreement, but more words did not bring about a peace treaty. The more we discussed it, the more hardened we became in our own perspectives.

To disagree over an issue is not an unusual problem in marriage because there are many issues that arise where you have a difference of perspective. But the way it usually worked for us is that in the course of a discussion, we both would give and take a little and, in the process, back away from insisting on our own point of view. Sometimes the solution was to just agree to disagree, like an uncommunicated peace treaty. The terms of the unwritten agreement made it possible to talk about the issue without instantly becoming angry and heated. What I am trying to say is that Tom and I had learned to agreeably disagree with each other on many things.

However, we could not even agree to disagree this time. We each kept contending for our point of view, and neither of us would back away from it. We would talk and talk and talk about our perspective but never come to a solution. After weeks of the same argument we had said everything there was to say, and we still could not agree in a way that would allow us to find peace. It was exhausting.

One day we were starting to go around that mountain one more time when I said, "Tom, let's just stop right now. Let's pretend we have already had the discussion where you say the same things you've been saying every time we talk about this and I say the same things I've already said a hundred times. Now let's skip past all those hurt feelings and angry emotions that build up when we argue about this and fast-forward to the end of the argument, where we still don't agree with each other and nothing has changed. OK? That way we can end the discussion and we don't have to feel completely drained. Now can we talk about something else?"

We agreed to table it and move on to something else. We had never resolved conflict this way before, but we had never had an issue that produced a standoff like this one. After that each time the issue surfaced in our conversation, we would just look at each other and say, "You know," and dismiss the conversation without erupting into an argument. To say the least, it was an uneasy truce.

This was a temporary solution to stop the destruction that angry words bring, but it did not help us resolve the issue. It just prevented us from doing more damage to each other. It really bugged us, though, that there was this *thing* that constantly came between us. After being together for four decades, we were stumped as to what to do next! We could not figure out how to get past it. We had a good marriage and loved each other, but we had used every tool in our relational toolbox and had nothing in it to help us fix the problem. We had prayed with each other and especially for each other, but there was no agreement to be found.

We talked about getting help and began to consider outside counseling. This was not an easy decision because it felt weak and embarrassing to admit that we couldn't handle this problem on our own with God. We believed in counseling—we had recommended it over and over again for other people. We had been able to navigate through hard times in our marriage before by being in Bible study and small groups, listening to good teaching, going to marriage seminars, being in Bible study groups, reading good books, and talking with friends. We had been the ones who gave counseling, not received it…until now.

We have a friend in the ministry who had gone to see a family counselor in our area, so we got his name and made an appointment to see him. We went with high hopes that he could help us fix the problem. We spent a couple of hours talking to him and set up a series of sessions as follow-up for us to begin regular counseling in the weeks to come.

Afterward when we got back in the car, Tom said, "Well, that was good."

I said, "Are you kidding? I don't feel like he helped us at all. He didn't give us anything we can use right now. I feel like I went to the emergency room with a broken arm and he gave me a bandage and an aspirin and told me to come back in a week."

We had agreed before we started counseling that if one or both of us did not connect with the counselor, we would not continue with that counselor but would continue looking for another one until we found a counselor who worked for both of us. So we decided since I wasn't comfortable that we would not to go back to him.

The next week I was talking to a friend and she gave me the name of someone she thought could help us. I called and made an appointment. As Tom and I discussed our scheduled appointment, he told me that when we met with the counselor, we needed to be totally candid with him, with both of us giving the full details of our perspective so he could make the right assessment—one of us was wrong and needed to change. He asked if I would be willing to change if it was determined that I was wrong. I said I was willing, and he said he was too.

We saw the counselor individually for a couple of sessions, and I was helped immediately while Tom was cautiously optimistic. He was antsy to learn who was right and who was wrong. We began seeing good results when we started meeting together with the counselor. I think I could write a book about all the stuff we learned from him because he helped us so much.

One of the first things he told us was that the goal of our counseling was to discover what God was saying to us, not to determine or discuss who was right or wrong. He told us we both had valid perspectives and that his goal was to blend and connect our perspectives.

Wow! No one was wrong? That was a novel idea and totally took the issue out of the "right versus wrong" arena, which freed us up to be able to hear what each other was saying without defending our own position. We were given new tools to help us in our communication. Better yet, we quit arguing about the issue and began reconnecting with each other. Over the next year our issue became a nonissue as our hearts healed and reconnected.

So often we are too ashamed or too proud to admit we need outside help as we seek to address the problems we are facing.

It feels like it is a sign of being weak or unspiritual to ask for help. Tom and I didn't realize we felt that way until we were the ones who needed help. But we were desperate to get help, so we let go of our pride and committed ourselves to the process of counseling to overcome this barrier that was between us. We were helped so much by counseling that we totally changed our minds related to our own personal need for counseling. We are now big advocates for people in leadership to seek a good counselor for help when they are having issues they can't solve with their own skillful effort. We encourage anyone who is having relational issues that they just can't resolve to get help—no matter who they are or what their level of spiritual maturity. Professional counseling can be a great source of help for our marriages.

It is not a badge of honor to say that you have never needed counseling, nor is it a badge of shame to say that you have gone to counseling. It takes courage and vulnerability to share your private pain with someone else. We are not ashamed that we got help. We freely tell any couple who is struggling and cannot get past their issues that good counseling can help. We hope that by sharing our experience, we will take away the embarrassment or shame you might feel related to seeking counseling.

Not every disagreement requires a trip to see the counselor, just as every sniffle does not require a visit to the doctor. However, when you have done all you know to do to address the problem and you still can't find a satisfying solution, we encourage people to seek counseling before the molehill becomes a mountain. We want you to get the help you need to strengthen your marriage, whether you've been married one year or sixty years.

One other thought related to counseling. Maybe, like our initial counseling experience, you have gone for counseling and you weren't helped. Maybe through your counseling experience you have become discouraged and feel hopeless. I want to encourage you not to lose hope, no matter how difficult your issue may seem to be. There is help for you, so do not be discouraged. If you have tried counseling with someone and they haven't helped you, try somebody else.

Then when you find someone who is helping you, don't jump ship when things start to get a little difficult. Your counselor may say some things that are hard to hear, and there will probably be some uncomfortable conversations and self-revelations that you will have to deal with. A good counselor will help you see things and deal with things that you could not deal with on your own. They will not tear you down but will encourage you and help guide you along the path to a healthy relationship. We have to be willing and committed to stay engaged in the process and do our part to produce a strong, healthy relationship.

Flourishing Through Spiritual Connection

❧ Tom ❧

Some people would be satisfied if they could just achieve emotional and physical connection with their spouse. However, if you stop there, you will miss a key ingredient in creating a satisfying marriage: spiritual connection.

Spiritual connection provides a depth and unity between two people that identifies and blends the unique purpose of both individuals in the marriage. At its core, spiritual connection reflects the knowledge that God created us for relationship with Him and that He has a purpose for our lives and our marriages. In fact, marriage was His idea!

Spiritual connection has to begin with both parties having a personal relationship with God. Our individual spiritual connection reflects a pursuit of Him and a desire to fulfill His purpose. Developing spiritual connection in marriage involves combining our individual pursuit of His purpose with the intimacy we are working to develop in our marriage.

The degree of our spiritual connection is determined by our openness to share and discuss what we know and are experiencing about God and His purposes for our lives individually and as a couple. This requires a willingness to share frustrations, questions, and desires freely with each other without judging each other. Pursuit and discovery of God's purpose together with support and encouragement given to each other will determine the depth of spiritual connection we will have in our marriage.

My first awareness of what I now know was spiritual disconnection happened in the early years of our marriage. We were at a Christmas party with a group of couples from our church. We were playing the newlywed game. This is a fun ice-breaker where four couples are selected and the spouses are separated from each other and asked questions their spouses will have to answer, hopefully correctly, as a reflection of how well they know each other.

We were asked a variety of questions designed to test our knowledge of each other—questions such as, What is your husband's favorite sport? What is your wife's favorite perfume? Where was your first date? What is your favorite food? The couple with the most correct answers wins the game.

One of the questions exposed an area of insecurity, as it revealed a spiritual disconnection in our relationship. The question was, "How many times a week do you pray with your wife?" One by one each of my friends answered the question with little hesitation. Their answers seemed so godly and spiritual compared to mine. I was intimidated and embarrassed to give a truthful answer. I struggled to determine how I would answer the question. Jan and I prayed together over our meals, and we prayed together over big decisions, but we didn't actually have a specific prayer time together. One by one my friends gave their answers—three, five seven—and then it was my turn. The truthful answer in my mind was zero. Jan had a different answer that reflected a different perspective than mine. I remember being humiliated and thinking I needed to do something more in my spiritual connection with her.

Before that night I would not have said we were spiritually disconnected. We went to church together and attended Bible study together, but this question exposed an area where I was insecure. There were certain aspects of my relationship with God that I held separate from Jan, not out of meanness or hurt but more out of insecurity and a lack of awareness than anything else. Through an introspection that began that night surrounding the question of prayer, I realized our spiritual connection was not as deep as it could have been with a little more focused effort and emotional openness on my part.

I was hesitant to become vulnerable enough to pray with Jan over everyday issues in our life. I could pray over specific things, such as asking God to bless our meals or to help us make a decision over what job to take or where to live. But praying over nothing specific, just praying about things that might bubble out of my heart—What would I say? How would I say it? What if I didn't do it right or my prayer came out sounding funny? These are hurdles I realized I had to overcome to begin connecting with Jan in a deeper spiritual way.

God has created us for spiritual connection with Him. I believe every person is searching for a spiritual connection that only God can fulfill. When we marry, that search for spiritual connection broadens to include our wives in that search. Our desire for a healthy marriage involves seeking spiritual connection first with God and then with our spouses, as we reflect our relationship with Him in our marriage.

The place to begin is to ask yourself these questions: Are you personally pursuing God? Are you willing to share your pursuit of God and His purpose for your life with your spouse? This openness is what will create a foundation that will enable a deeper spiritual connection between the two of you.

One of the many benefits of a spiritual connection is that it provides a solid foundation for raising a family and dealing with the issues of life. It also provides God's strength as we work to build and sustain a lifetime marriage partnership with each other because we understand that our relationship is about more than just ourselves. It is worth the effort to make a spiritual connection with your spouse because it will open your relationship to a whole new level of connection and intimacy—not to mention the expanded partnership with God.

Let's Talk About You

I don't want you to be discouraged or frustrated if you're not experiencing any of this. I can tell you that you will never arrive at a place of complete physical, emotional, and spiritual connection with your spouse. The deeper your relationship grows, the more capacity gets created in these areas for even greater relational connection. It is our prayer that this chapter has encouraged you to want to diligently pursue intimacy with your spouse and to develop your connection across all the levels we have been discussing. We hope it has given you a vision and a framework for understanding your relational connection as you work together to develop the amazing marriage that God intended for you!

Chapter 13

WHERE TO FROM HERE?

N November 1943 twelve American nurses boarded a transport plane in Sicily. They were scheduled for a short flight to southern Italy, where they would continue their work caring for injured American soldiers fighting in the area. But their plane was attacked by German fighters and blown off course into a terrible storm. The pilot was forced to crash land, and the thirty survivors, including the nurses, were shocked to learn that they were hundreds of miles off course in the Nazi-occupied Albania.

Aware that Nazis would soon be on site to take them prisoner, the crew fled the plane. The women could have surrendered and, as female noncombatants, expected to be treated relatively well. But they would have none of that. They instead embarked on a dangerous journey behind enemy lines, taking shelter with local resistance fighters as they made their way along the coast, hoping to connect with Allied Forces and ultimately be rescued.

They walked almost eight hundred miles through hostile territory, often barely keeping ahead of Nazi forces. They climbed an eight thousand-foot mountain during a blizzard, survived enemy gunfire, and escaped a town of resisters moments before German forces leveled it. Eventually the group made contact with British Intelligence and arranged to be evacuated. Amazingly all thirty who survived the plane crash made it out safely.[1]

This story may seem like an unusual place to begin our final chapter together. However, it gives an image of the kind of journey for survival your marriage may be encountering. Every couple who desires to build a lifetime marriage, especially one that is heart connected and mutually satisfying, is in a battle. The battle isn't one of the sexes, nor is it a battle between people with different personalities. Those are just the surface skirmishes. The underlying battle is a spiritual confrontation between the unseen forces that war against us in an effort to keep us from experiencing all that God has for us.

Your marriage plane was loaded with supplies, fuel, and all that was needed when it took off on your wedding day. It was headed toward the intended destination of wedded bliss, marital satisfaction, and fulfilling family life, but it came under attack and was blown off course by the storms of life. It may be that your marriage is still flying in what you believe is the right direction, and you are unaware that challenges are waiting ahead. Or you may have lost your bearings as you navigate your marriage through the challenges of life. Or maybe you're in a more serious situation, and your marriage has taken a route that has brought you under such pressure and enemy fire that it is going down in smoke and you feel the panic of an impending crash in your relationship. Or perhaps as you have read this book you are fully aware that your marriage has more than flown off course; it has crashed, and you are trying to find your way to a place of rescue.

Just like the twelve American nurses and the other eighteen passengers on that transport flight during World War II, you can survive the difficult circumstances you are experiencing and make it to a place of rescue! Survival in difficult circumstances has everything to do with the will to live coupled with faith in God's unfailing care. There are numerous amazing and awe-inspiring testimonies of marriages that survived difficult circumstances.

It has been our desire to build hope in you and equip you by telling you more than a story of survival. Jan and I have told our experiences as we have journeyed to building a lifelong, heart-connected marriage. Our purpose has been to motivate you and inspire you to not give up—to not lose hope but to have faith to keep pressing on toward a rescue for your marriage. As you face the situations your marriage is encountering, we have sought to encourage you to press on by shedding light on the relational issues we had to overcome. Our perspective on situations in our marriage has been from the dynamic of an aggressive, passionate, strong woman and a passive, reserved, quiet man, and the way we have overcome obstacles as we built an intimate and satisfying marriage.

Don't let the brokenness of your marriage or the difficult circumstances that surround you overwhelm you to the point of giving up. It is good and necessary for you to make a determined response that will not allow the brokenness you have experienced to continue. Survival is dependent upon you not staying where you are today. From this place of faith and determination, take the steps that are needed to ensure your marriage gets to a place of rescue, healing, and, ultimately, thriving. You are not alone in your journey. Jan and I, along with many others, are behind your efforts. We are praying for, believing for, and supporting your commitment to the process, and we know that your efforts will bring you to the place of a healthy, growing, heart-connected, intimate relationship with your spouse.

A Word About Abuse

Before we say good-bye, we feel compelled to talk about an area we haven't touched on yet. That is the topic of abuse. If you are experiencing any kind of abuse in your marriage, your marriage has not only crashed but you have also sustained life-threatening injuries. Your injuries may be so extensive that they have impaired you emotionally, physically, and spiritually. You have been traumatized, and whether you realize it or not, you have barely survived the crash. In a situation like this you are not able to get yourself to the place of help and rescue. What should you do? You need to get help!

If you are experiencing physical abuse, you need to take steps immediately to protect yourself. Whether this has just begun or has been going on for some time, you need to get out of the abusive situation. Don't deny it or make excuses for it. Get out! It is important that you not wait until there is another incident. If you have children, take them and go to a rescue shelter as you sort things out. You must remove yourself and your children from the person who is abusing you. It will be very hard and scary to take that step, but your life and future generations depend on you taking this step. You cannot evaluate your situation clearly in the midst of a dangerous situation, and you need professional help to guide you through the steps necessary to protect your life and the lives of your children.

You need to learn a way of life that does not tolerate the degradation that abuse imposes. And please do not let the person who has abused you talk you into staying in that situation with words of sorrow or promises to change that go unfulfilled as the abuse continues.

Abuse is never your fault. You may have come to accept it or tolerate it for many reasons, but you need to become strong and healthy with help from a professional. Then you can view your situation from a perspective of health and strength to make decisions for your future.

Get professional and pastoral help to guide you in your rescue-recovery process. You need help and support to leave this lifestyle. There is hope for you! Miraculous change can happen, but it will begin by you taking a bold and brave step to stop your physical abuse. You can start by calling the National Domestic Violence Hotline at 1-800-799-7233; it is available 24/7 and is completely confidential.

The more difficult kind of abuse to recognize is emotional abuse. There are no physical bruises or scars to show for it, so you may not even know it is happening to you. We have talked with individuals through the years who have become unhappy and discouraged by the circumstances of their relationship. A woman may feel ignored, used, belittled, and like nothing more than a cook, bottle washer, nanny, and bed partner for the uncaring, manipulative, selfish man she married. A man may feel belittled, unappreciated, dishonored, and like nothing more than a cash cow for the selfish, uncaring, manipulative woman he married. With these feelings flavoring every encounter between them, their exchanges become more and more angry and hurtful. Withdrawal, invalidation, and cynicism all become part of the emotional mix of the relationship, and the self-diagnosis is emotional abuse.

We have no doubt that everything taking place has an emotional impact on both parties, but is it emotional abuse? It is dysfunctional and needs to change, but is it abuse? Is it serious enough that you need to take action to protect yourself, or is it an excuse to get out of your unhappy marriage? The only way to really know is to go to an outside source such as a pastor or professional counselor and honestly expose the pattern that exists in your relationship that makes you feel abused.

If you are convinced that you are experiencing emotional abuse, get professional help. By professional help I mean a licensed counselor, preferably one with a Christian worldview—not just a close relative or trusted Christian friend. Most often it is difficult for a family member or friend to avoid becoming offended and biased by what they have heard or observed in your relationship. When they are aware of your pain, it clouds their ability to give the best guidance for making a decision with such life-impacting consequences. So if you feel you are experiencing emotional abuse, get qualified counseling help to guide you in your situation. Don't allow the emotional abuse to continue or escalate to the point of causing your marriage to crash!

THE MARRIAGE OF YOUR DREAMS

Like those in the story I shared at the beginning of this chapter, you can overcome extreme and difficult circumstances on your way to rescue, healing, and, ultimately, the relationship you desire. God is your partner in the process. Press in to Him, depend upon Him, and allow Him to do miraculous things along the way. Keep your focus on what you need to do for survival rather than on the immediate circumstances, and continue your work toward getting help and healing.

Jan and I are praying that what we have shared in this book has furthered and supported God's work in you and your desire to live out your commitment to each other and build a happy, fulfilling marriage. Our desire is to give you hope and encouragement that you can keep growing and learning new ways to connect with each other.

We leave you with this amazing passage from Scripture:

> Now to Him who is able to do exceedingly abundantly beyond all that we ask or imagine, according to the power that works in us.
>
> —EPHESIANS 3:20, MEV

APPENDIX

❧

HE FOLLOWING RESOURCES ARE RECOMMENDED to you to help address sexual issues in your marriage. They are biblically based books from respected authors who are recognized experts in this area of marriage development.

Gregoire, Sheila Wray. *The Good Girl's Guide to Great Sex.* Grand Rapids, MI: Zondervan, 2012.

Langberg, Diane. *On the Threshold of Hope: Opening the Door to Healing for Survivors of Sexual Abuse.* Forest, VA: American Association of Christian Counselors, 1999.

Lasser, Mark. *Healing the Wounds of Sexual Addiction.* Grand Rapids, MI: Zondervan, 2004.

Parrott, Les. *Crazy Good Sex.* Grand Rapids, MI: Zondervan, 2011.

Penner, Clifford L. and Joyce J. Penner. *Getting Your Sex Life Off to a Great Start.* Nashville: Thomas Nelson, 1994.

———. *Sex Facts for the Family.* Nashville: W Publishing Group, 1992.

———. *The Gift of Sex.* Nashville: W Publishing Group, 2003.

————. *The Way to Love Your Wife.* Carol Stream, IL: Focus on the Family, 2007.

Rosenau, Douglas E. *A Celebration of Sex.* Nashville: Thomas Nelson, 2002.

Rosenau, Douglas E. and Jim and Carolyn Childerston. *A Celebration of Sex After 50.* Nashville: Thomas Nelson, 2004.

Tracy, Steven. *Mending the Soul.* Grand Rapids, MI: Zondervan, 2005.

Tracy, Steven and Celestia. *Mending the Soul Workbook for Men and Women.* N.p.: n.d.

NOTES

CHAPTER 1
UNCOVERING THE PASSIVE MAN

1.   Scott Wetzler, *Living With the Passive-Aggressive Man* (New York: Fireside, 1992), 14.

2.   Ibid., 16.

3.   *American Heritage Dictionary*, s.v. "passive," https://www.ahdictionary.com/word/search.html?q=passive&submit.x=33&submit.y=34 (accessed October 6, 2014).

CHAPTER 3
THE THIEF THAT DESTROYS

1.   Pat Springle, *Codependency* (Houston: Rapha Publishing, 1990).

2.   Margaret Rinck, *Can Christians Love Too Much?* (Grand Rapids, MI: Zondervan, 1990).

CHAPTER 11
FINDING RESOLUTION

1.   John M. Gottman and Nan Silver, *The Seven Principles for Making Marriage Work* (New York: Three Rivers Press, 1999), 23.

2.   John Gottman, *Why Marriages Succeed or Fail* (New York: Simon & Schuster, 1994), 28.

3.   Ibid.

4.   Howard J. Markman, Scott M. Stanley, and Susan L. Blumberg, *Fighting for Your Marriage: Positive Steps for Preventing Divorce and Preserving a Lasting Love* (San Francisco: Jossey-Bass, 2001), 37.

CHAPTER 13
WHERE TO FROM HERE?

1.   Alex Hanton, "10 Epic Tales of Survival Against All Odds," ListVerse, July 8, 2014, http://listverse.com/2014/07/08/10-epic-tales-of-survival-against-all-odd (accessed October 19, 2014); Agnes Jensen Mangerich, *Albanian Escape: The True Story of U.S. Army Nurses Behind Enemy Lines* (Lexington, KY: The University Press of Kentucky, 1999).

5-16